The Mind Doesn't Work That Way

Representation and Mind
Hilary Putnam and Ned Block, editors

The Mind Doesn't Work That Way

The Scope and Limits of Computational Psychology

Jerry Fodor

A Bradford Book
The MIT Press
Cambridge, Massachusetts
London, England

Second printing, 2000

© 2000 Massachusetts Institute of Technology

This book was set in Palatino by The MIT Press and was printed and bound in the United States of America.

Library of Congress Cataloging-in-Publication Data

Fodor, Jerry A.
  The mind doesn't work that way : the scope and limits of computational psychology / Jerry Fodor.
    p.   cm. — (Representation and mind)
  "A Bradford book."
  Includes bibliographical references and author index.
  ISBN 0-262-06212-7 (hc : alk. paper)
  1. Cognitive science. 2. Philosophy of mind. 3. Nativism (Psychology). I. Title. II. Series.
BD418.3 .F627   2000
153—dc21   99-089687

For Greycat, who was my friend, who helped me to write this, and whom I miss very much.

I'm thinking, I'm thinking.
—Jack Benny

It seems probable that if we were never bewildered there would never be a story to tell about us.
—Henry James

Contents

Acknowledgments

In its first incarnation, this book was a series of three lectures presented in the summer of 1997 to the Facolta di Psicologia, Università San Raffale, under the sponsorship of the Sigma Tau Foundation. I'm grateful to an old Italian friend, Professor Massimo Piatelli, for having arranged the occasion; to many new Italian friends for comments and criticism; and to Dr. Donata Vercelli for having steered me through a traumatic loss of credit cards, the ultimate Jamesian crisis for an American abroad.

All of the following did me the great kindness of reading through earlier versions of part or all of the manuscript and helping me to catch the mistakes. Much gratitude to: Ned Block, Noam Chomsky, Shaun Nichols, Zenon Pylyshyn, and Stephen Stich.

The appendix was first published in *Cognition*. Permission to reprint is gratefully acknowledged.

Not one red cent was contributed to the support of this work by: The MacArthur Foundation, the McDonnell Pugh Foundation, the National Science Foundation, or the National Institutes of Health.

The author is listed alphabetically.

List of Abbreviations

The following abbreviations occur in the text:

CDM	Cheater Detection Module
CTM	Computational Theory of Mind
E(CTM)	CTM conjoined with principle E
GLT	General Linguistic Theory
M(CTM)	Minimal Computational Theory of Mind (The role of a mental representation in a cognitive process supervenes on some syntactic facts or other)
MM(T)	Massive modularity (thesis)
MR	Mental representation
MP	Modus ponens
Principle E	Only essential properties of a mental representation can determine its causal role in mental life.
RTM	Representational Theory of Mind

Introduction: Still Snowing

Over the years, I've written a number of books in praise of the Computational Theory of Mind (CTM often hereinafter). It is, in my view, by far the best theory of cognition that we've got; indeed, the only one we've got that's worth the bother of a serious discussion. There are facts about the mind that it accounts for and that we would be utterly at a loss to explain without it; and its central idea—that intentional processes are syntactic operations defined on mental representations—is strikingly elegant. There is, in short, every reason to suppose that the Computational Theory is part of the truth about cognition.[1]

But it hadn't occurred to me that anyone could think that it's a very *large* part of the truth; still less that it's within miles of being the whole story about how the mind works. (Practitioners of artificial intelligence have sometimes said things that suggest they harbor such convictions. But, even by its own account, AI was generally supposed to be about engineering, not about science; and certainly not about philosophy.) So, then, when I wrote books about what a fine thing CTM is, I generally made it a point to include a section saying that I don't suppose that it could comprise more than a fragment of a full and satisfactory cognitive psychology; and that the most interesting—certainly the hardest—problems about thinking are unlikely to be much illuminated by any kind of computational theory we are now able to imagine. I guess I sort of took it for granted that even us ardent admirers of computational psychology were more or less agreed on that.

I am now, however, disabused of taking that for granted. A couple of years ago, *The London Review of Books* asked me to write about two new publications, each of which summarized and commended a theory that is increasingly influential in cognitive science: Steven Pinker's *How the Mind Works* and Henry Plotkin's *Evolution in Mind*. These books suggest, in quite similar terms, how one might combine CTM with a comprehensive psychological nativism and with biological principles borrowed from a neo-Darwinist account of evolution. Pinker's and Plotkin's view appears to be that the resulting synthesis, even if it doesn't quite constitute a general map of the cognitive mind, is pretty much the whole story about large areas of Manhattan, the Bronx, and Staten Island. I thought both books admirable and authoritative in many respects; but, though I'm a committed—not to say fanatical—nativist myself, I wasn't entirely happy with either, and I said so in my review.[2]

For one thing, although they accurately set out a network of doctrines about the cognitive mind that many nativists hold, neither book makes as explicit as I thought it might have how the various strands fit together. For a second thing, though neither book spends a lot of time on the alternatives, the Pinker/Plotkin view is by no means the only kind of current cognitive science that's friendly to the idea that lots of knowledge is innate. Indeed, Noam Chomsky, who is surely as close to personifying the nativist revival as anybody can get, is nevertheless quite out of sympathy with much of what Pinker and Plotkin endorse. Readers who are new to the cognitive science game may well find this puzzling, but I hope to make it clear as we go along what the disagreement is about. Third, both books insist on a connection between nativism about cognition and a neo-Darwinist, adaptationist account of how the cognitive mind evolved. That struck me as neither convincingly argued in the texts nor particularly plausible in its own right. Finally, I was, and remain, perplexed by an attitude of ebullient optimism that's particularly characteristic of Pinker's book. As just remarked, I would have thought that the last forty or fifty years have demonstrated pretty clearly that there are aspects of higher mental processes into which the current armamentarium of computational models, theories, and experimental techniques offers vanishingly little insight. And I would have thought that all of this is common knowledge in the trade. How, in light of it, could any-body manage to be so relentlessly cheerful?

So, it occurred to me to write a book of my own. I had it in mind to pick up some old threads in passing; in particular, I wanted to extend a discussion of the modularity (or otherwise) of cognitive architecture that I'd first embarked upon a million years or so ago in (Fodor 1983). But the book I thought I'd write would be mostly about the status of computational nativism in cognitive science. And it would be much shorter, and much more jaundiced, than either Pinker's or Plotkin's. The shortness would be mostly because, unlike them, I wasn't going to write an intro-ductory text, or to review the empirical cognitive science litera-ture, or even to argue in much detail for the account of the field I would propose. I'd be satisfied just to articulate a geography of the issues that's quite different from the map that Pinker and Plotkin have on offer. The jaundice would be mostly in the con-clusion: Computational nativism is clearly the best theory of the cognitive mind that anyone has thought of so far (vastly better than, for example, the associationistic empiricism that is the main alternative); and there may indeed be aspects of cognition about which computational nativism has got the story more or less right. But it's nonetheless quite plausible that computational nativism is, in large part, not true.

In the fullness of time, I embarked upon that project, but the more I wrote, the unhappier I became. I'd started off intending to take CTM more or less for granted as the background theory and to concentrate on issues about nativism and adaptationism. But in the event, that turned out not to be feasible; perhaps unsur-prisingly, what one says about any of these matters depends very much on what one thinks about the others.

There are many claims about nativism, and about adaptation-ism, in the book I ended up with (and which, I trust, you have just purchased). But part of the context for discussing them is an attempt to get clearer on what's right, and what's wrong, about the idea that the mind is a computer.[3]

The cognitive science that started fifty years or so ago more or less explicitly[4] had as its defining project to examine a theory, largely owing to Turing, that cognitive mental processes are operations defined on syntactically structured mental representations that are much like sentences.[5] The proposal was to use the hypothesis that mental representations are languagelike to explain certain pervasive and characteristic properties of cognitive states and processes; for example, that the former are productive and systematic, and that the latter are, by and large, truth preserving. Roughly, the systematicity and productivity of thought were supposed to trace back to the compositionality of mental representations, which in turn depends on their syntactic constituent structure. The tendency of mental processes to preserve truth was to be explained by the hypothesis that they are computations, where by stipulation a computation is a causal process that is syntactically driven.[6]

I think that the attempt to explain the productivity and systematicity of mental states by appealing to the compositionality of mental representations has been something like an unmitigated success;[7] in my view, it amply vindicates the postulation of a language of thought. That, however, is a twice-told tale, and I won't dwell on it in the discussion that follows. By contrast, it seems to me that the attempt to reduce thought to computation has had a decidedly mixed career. It's a consolation, however, that there is much to be learned both from its successes and from its failures. Over the last forty years or so, we've been putting questions about cognitive processes to Nature, and Nature has been replying with interpretable indications of the scope and limits of the computational theory of the cognitive mind. The resultant pattern is broadly intelligible; so, at least, I am going to claim.

Before the discussion gets seriously under way, however, I want to sketch a brief overview for purposes of orientation. Here, in a nutshell, is what I think Nature has been trying to tell us about the scope and limits of the computational model:

It's been pretty clear since Freud, that our pretheoretical, "folk" taxonomy of mental states conflates two quite different natural kinds: the intrinsically *intentional* ones, of which beliefs, desires, and the like are paradigms;[8] and the intrinsically *con-

scious ones, of which sensations, feelings, and the like are para-digms.[9,10] Likewise, I claim, a main result of the attempt to fit the facts of human cognition to the classical, Turing account of com-putation is that we need a comparably fundamental dichotomy between mental processes that are *local* and ones that aren't. There is (I continue to claim) a characteristic cluster of properties that typical examples of local mental processes reliably share with one another but not with typical instances of global ones.[11] Three of these features are most pertinent to our purposes: Local mental processes appear to accommodate pretty well to Turing's theory that thinking is computation; they appear to be largely modular; and much of their architecture, and of what they know about their proprietary domains of application, appears to be innately specified.

By contrast, what we've found out about global cognition is mainly that it is different from the local kind in all three of these respects; and that, because it is, we deeply do not understand it. Since the mental processes thus afflicted with globality appar-ently include some of the ones that are most characteristic of human cognition, I'm on balance not inclined to celebrate how much we have so far learned about how our minds work. The bottom line will be that the current situation in cognitive science is light years from being satisfactory. Perhaps somebody will fix it eventually; but not, I should think, in the foreseeable future, and not with the tools that we currently have in hand. As he so often does, Eeyore catches the mood exactly: "'It's snowing still,' said Eeyore, '. . . and freezing. . . . However,' he said, brightening up a little, 'we haven't had an earthquake lately.'"

This, then, is the itinerary: In chapter 1, I set out some of the main ideas that are currently in play in nativistic discussions of cognition. In particular, I want to distinguish the synthesis of nativism, computational psychology, and (neo-)Darwinism that Pinker and Plotkin both endorse from Chomsky's story about innateness. Chomskian nativism and this New Synthesis[12] are, in some respects, quite compatible. But as we'll see, they are also in some respects quite different; and even when they endorse the same slogans, it's often far from clear that they mean the same things by them. For example, Chomskian nativists and computational nativists both view themselves as inheriting the tradition of philosophical rationalism, but they do so for rather different reasons. Chomsky's account (so I'll suggest) is primarily responsive to questions about the sources and uses of knowledge, and so continues the tradition of rationalist *epistemology*. Computational nativism, by contrast, is primarily about the nature of mental *processes* (like thinking, for example) and so continues the tradition of rationalist *psychology*.

I expect that much of what I'll have to say in the first chapter will be familiar to old hands, and I'd skip it if I could. However, standard accounts of New Synthesis cognitive psychology (including, notably, both Pinker's and Plotkin's) often hardly mention what seems to me be overwhelmingly its determining feature, namely, its commitment to Turing's *syntactic* account of mental processes. Leaving that out simplifies the exposition, to be sure; but it's Hamlet without the Prince. I propose to put the Prince back even though, here as in the play, doing so makes no end of trouble for everyone concerned. Much of this book will be about how the idea that cognitive processes are syntactic shapes the New Synthesis story; and why I doubt that the syntactic theory of mental processes could be anything like the whole truth about cognition, and what we're left with if it's not.

The second chapter will discuss what I take to be the limitations of the syntactic account of the mental, and chapter 3 will consider some ways in which computational nativists have tried, in my view not successfully, to evade these limitations. In chapter 4, the currently fashionable "massive modularity thesis" will emerge as one such failed way out. The last chapter concerns the connection of all of this to issues about psychological Darwinism.

It will become clear, as the exposition proceeds, that I think some version of Chomskian nativism will probably turn out to be true and that the current version of New Synthesis nativism probably won't. I suspect that the basic perplexity of the New Synthesis is that the syntactic/computational theory of thought that it depends on is likely to hold for cognitive processes in general only if the architecture of the mind is mostly modular—which, however, there is good reason to suppose that it isn't. On the other hand, a tenable cognitive psychology does urgently need some theory of mental processes or other, and Chomsky rather clearly doesn't have one. So if computational nativism is radically untenable, Chomskian nativism is radically incomplete. Ah, well, nobody ever said that understanding the cognitive mind was going to be easy.

At least, I'm pretty sure that I never did. In fact, for whatever it may be worth, my views on these matters haven't changed much since I started writing about this sort of topic. It's the main point of the last chapter of *The Language of Thought* (1975) that the computational model is implausible as an account of global cognition. And it's a central theme in *The Modularity of Mind* (1983) that modular cognition is where Turing's computational story about mental processes is most likely to be true. Consistency over time isn't a virtue I generally care a lot about. In my experience, scientific progress (to say nothing of philosophical progress) is nonmonotonic as often as not. I admit, however, that the present doctrines are compatible with—indeed, that they mostly elaborate upon—several of my earlier attempts.

Finally, while I'm in this confessional mood, I should emphasize that what follows, though it proposes a reading of the recent history of cognitive science, isn't remotely a work of scholarship. Various familiar names (Eeyore, of course; but also Chomsky, Darwin, Hume, Kant, Plato, Turing, and others) will appear from time to time, and perhaps it goes without saying that I'll be pleased if I've reported their views more or less correctly. But my main concern is to explicate such options for a nativistic cognitive science as are currently visible, and I'll generally think of the distinguished persons we meet along the way much less as historical figures than as ideal types.

So then, to work at last.

Chapter 1

Varieties of Nativism

Chomsky's Nativism

The present phase of nativistic theorizing about the cognitive mind began with two suggestions of Noam Chomsky's: that there are substantive, universal constraints on the kinds of grammars that natural languages can have; and that these constraints express correspondingly substantive and universal properties of human psychology (determined, presumably, by the characteristic genetic endowment of our species). In effect, Chomsky predicted the convergence of two lines of research:

- On the one hand, empirical investigation of the range of grammatical structures that human languages exhibit would estimate the limits within which it is possible for them to vary. One then subtracts the ways that human languages can differ from the ways in which it is conceivable that languages *could* differ. The remainder after the subtraction is the set of linguistic universals that implicitly define "possible human language."[1]
- On the other hand, empirical investigations of the conditions under which children learn to talk would estimate the information their linguistic environments provide, hence how much poverty of the stimulus the language learning process tolerates. One then subtracts the information that is in the environment from the information that is required for the child to achieve linguistic mastery. The remainder after the subtraction is what the child's innate knowledge contributes to the language acquisition process.

If everything goes well, it should turn out that what the child innately knows will be the same universal principles that constrain the humanly possible languages. Such a convergence would explain, in one stroke, both why human languages don't differ *arbitrarily* and also why (pace occasional sentimental claims on behalf of dolphins and chimpanzees) only human beings seem to be any good at learning them.

In principle, the research strategy that Chomsky proposed seems perfectly straightforward to execute. One need only determine the empirical values of the relevant parameters, perform the indicated subtractions, and then compare the remainders. So why, you might wonder, didn't somebody just get a grant and do it? In practice that turned out not to be easy. For one thing, it's not easy for cognitive scientists to get grants if they are working on questions of any theoretical interest. (To ensure this is a main function of the institution of peer review.) And, for another thing, even rational people can disagree about how much, and in what ways, languages actually differ; and about whether the residual similarities might after all be "explained away" without resort to nativistic postulations (perhaps by appealing to historical or environmental factors, or to the functional properties that any language would need to have if it is to be expressive and efficient). Likewise, it is no small matter to figure out what information the child's linguistic environment makes available to the acquisition process; or how much of what it makes available the child actually exploits; or how much of what the child actually exploits he could have done without, consonant with achieving normal fluency by the normal means. One can't, of course, perform Kasper Hauser experiments on the offspring of one's conspecifics.

So the argument that Chomsky started all those years ago continues unabated. I assume its general outlines are familiar, and I won't rehearse them further here. What's most striking for our purposes is a point about his view that Chomsky has himself often emphasized: Insofar as it concerns the relation between human language and human nature, his position is continuous with—indeed, practically indistinguishable from—one that philosophical rationalists have defended for centuries. Except for the characteristically modern identification of "human nature" with "what the human genotype specifies," Chomsky's ideas about innateness would have been intelligible to Plato; and they would have been intelligible in much the terms of the present debate.

This is because Chomsky's nativism is primarily a thesis about knowledge and belief; it aligns problems in the theory of language with those in the theory of knowledge. Indeed, as often as not, the vocabulary in which Chomsky frames linguistic issues is explicitly epistemological. Thus, the grammar of a language specifies what its speaker/hearers have to *know* qua speakers and hearers; and the goal of the child's language acquisition process is to construct a *theory* of the language that correctly expresses this grammatical knowledge. Likewise, the central problem of language acquisition arises from the poverty of the "primary linguistic *data*" from which the child effects this construction; and the proposed solution of the problem is that much of the knowledge that linguistic competence depends on is available to the child *a priori* (i.e., prior to learning). Everything I've put in italics belongs to the epistemologist's vocabulary; it is, to repeat, primarily epistemological nativism that Chomsky shares with the rationalists. When Plato asks what the slave boy knows about geometry, and where on earth he could have learned it, it really is much the same question that Chomsky asks about what speaker/hearers know about their language and where on earth they could have learned that. There is, I think, no equivocation on the key terms.[2]

By contrast, New Synthesis psychological theories of the kind that Pinker and Plotkin espouse are typically about not *epistemic states* but *cognitive processes*; for example, the mental processes involved in thinking, learning, and perceiving. The key idea of New Synthesis psychology is that cognitive processes are *computational*; and the notion of computation thus appealed to borrows heavily from the foundational work of Alan Turing. A computation, according to this understanding, is a formal operation on syntactically structured representations. Accordingly, a mental process, qua computation, is a formal operation on syntactically structured mental representations. We'll return to this idea quite soon and at length. Suffice it, for the moment, that whereas Chomsky's rationalism consists primarily in nativism about the knowledge that cognitive capacities manifest, New Synthesis rationalism consists primarily in nativism about the computational mechanisms that exploit such knowledge for the purposes of cognition. To put it in a nutshell: *What's new about the New Synthesis is mostly the consequence of conjoining a rationalist epistemology with a syntactic notion of mental computation.*

The attempt to ground psychology in the idea that mental processes are computations is a main topic of the discussion to follow. I'm mostly interested in telling you what I think is right about this idea and what I think isn't. But first I have to tell you how it's supposed to work. This will take some fairly extended exegesis. Please do bear with me. Unlike epistemic nativism, computational nativism really is a new kind of rationalist theory; whereas Plato would have understood Chomsky well enough, I doubt that he would have understood Turing at all.

The New Synthesis

1. Computation
It's a remarkable fact that you can tell, just by looking at it, that any (declarative) sentence of the syntactic form P and Q ("John swims and Mary drinks," for example) is true if and only if P and Q are themselves both true; that is, that sentences of the form P *and* Q entail, and are entailed by, the corresponding sentences P, Q. To say that "you can tell this just by looking" is to claim that you don't have to know anything about what either P or Q *means* to see that these entailment relations hold, and that you also don't have to know anything about the nonlinguistic world.[3] This really is remarkable since, after all, it's what they mean, together with the facts about the nonlinguistic world, that decide whether P or Q *are* true.

This line of thought is often summarized by saying that some inferences are "formally valid," which is in turn to say that they hold just in virtue of the "syntax" of the sentences that enter into them.[4] It was Turing's great discovery that machines can be designed to evaluate any inference that is formally valid in that sense. That's because, although machines are awful at figuring out what things mean and aren't much better at figuring out what's going on in the world, you can build them so that they are quite good at detecting and responding to syntactic properties and relations. That, in turn, is because the syntax of a sentence reduces to the identity and arrangement of its elementary parts, and, at least in the artificial languages that machines compute in, these elementary parts and arrangements can be exhaustively itemized, and the machine specifically designed to detect them.

So: Turing showed us how to make a computing machine that will recognize any argument that is valid in virtue of its syntax; and the basic thesis of the new psychological synthesis is that cognitive mental processes are (perhaps exhaustively) constituted by the kinds of operations that such machines perform.

Notice, in particular, that the reliance on syntax is essential; it's *only* if the sufficient conditions for an inference to be truth preserving are syntactic that Turing guarantees that a machine is able to recognize its validity. So if, like New Synthesis theorists, you propose to co-opt Turing's account of the nature of computation for use in a cognitive psychology of thought, you will have to assume that *thoughts themselves have syntactic structure.* What's on offer at the price of this assumption is the prospect of a theory that explains how, in a variety of kinds of cases, mental processes can lead, reliably, from one true thought to another. That sounds to me like a bargain.[5]

Right; so much, for now, for Turing's account of computation. What has all this got to do with the rationalist tradition in psychology?

The New Synthesis Continued

2. *Rationalist psychology*

Rationalists are nativists practically by definition; by contrast, the rationalist consensus about the nature of mental processes is less than transparent to first impressions. Still, I think there is such a consensus, epitomized perhaps by Kant; and that it has its roots in Aristotle and reaches us via such of the Scholastics as William of Occam. If this were a work of scholarship, and if I were a scholar, I'd try to make some sort of case for these historical claims; but it's not, and I'm not, so I won't. Suffice it to make explicit what I take the main idea of rationalist psychology to be, and how I suppose that it connects with the Turing-style account of computation sketched above.

The main idea of rationalist psychology is that beliefs, desires, thoughts, and the like have logical forms, and that their logical forms are among the determinants of the roles they play in mental processes. For example, *John swims and Mary drinks* is a *conjunctive* belief, and that is why having it can lead one to infer that John swims; *there aren't any unicorns* is a *negative existential* belief, and that is why having it can lead one to the infer that Alfred is not a unicorn. And so forth. Accordingly, I will use the term "rationalist psychology" for any theory according to which (at least some) mental states have logical form, and the causal role of a mental state depends (at least inter alia) on what logical form it has.[6]

What follows is a number of exegetical comments on the general character of rationalist psychologies so construed, and on why they accommodate themselves naturally to the thesis that mental processes are computations. We'll see that what connects the two is primarily the idea that the logical form of a thought might be reconstructed by the syntax of a mental representation that expresses it.

Comments (in no particular order):

- Beliefs, desires, thoughts, and the like[7] (from here on, I'll call them all "propositional attitudes") have their logical forms *intrinsically*. Which is to say not only that if x and y are propositional attitudes of different logical forms they are ipso facto different mental particulars, but also that they are ipso facto mental particulars of different types. Sam's belief that $P \lor Q$, for example, is ipso facto of a different type than his belief that $\sim(\sim P \& \sim Q)$, even though the two are, of course, logically equivalent.

• Propositional attitudes with different *contents* may have the same logical form. The belief that there isn't any Santa Clause has the same logical form as the belief that there aren't any unicorns even though they are, of course, different beliefs.

• Assume, for simplicity of exposition, that the paradigmatic propositional attitude is a belief that a certain individual has a certain property, for example, *that John is bald.* Such a belief has the logical form *Fa,* where "*F*" expresses the property that the individual is believed to have (e.g., being bald) and "*a*" specifies the individual that is believed to have that property (e.g., John). A belief of the form *Fa* is true if and only if the individual in question actually does have the property in question.

• As in the preceding example, so too in the general case: Propositional attitudes are complex objects; propositional attitudes have parts. In what follows, I'll often refer to the parts of a propositional attitude as its "constituents." The constituents of the belief that John is bald include: the part that expresses the property of being bald and the part that specifies John. In the psychologist's usage, the constituents of propositional attitudes are often called "concepts."[8]

• The logical form of a propositional attitude is not (repeat: is *not)* reducible to the causal relations among its constituents (which is not to deny that it may be reducible to some causal relations or other). *This is a fundamental difference between rationalist and empiricist psychologies:* whereas, according to the latter, the structure of a thought is fully determined by specifying the pattern of associations among its constituents, according to the former, it is an independent parameter.[9] It is basically because rationalists distinguish between the structure of a thought and what is sometimes called its degree of "associative integration" that they can explain how it is possible to come to believe the very same thing that one used to doubt or deny (or vice versa.)

I want to be as clear as I can about this, since I take it to be what primarily distinguishes computational psychology from the (connectionistic) associationism that is the main current alternative. Suppose I only *sort* of think that John is bald, whereas you are utterly certain that he is. Suppose, moreover, that it really matters to you whether John is bald, whereas I don't actually much care. In that case, your thinking *John* might cause you to think *bald* (or *he's bald*) with absolutely mechanical regularity, whereas my thinking *John* might cause me to think *bald* at most only now and then, or even not at all. Still, according to the present view, your thought that John is bald is a propositional attitude of exactly the same type as mine, and so a fortiori, they have the same logical form. So, to repeat, its logical form and the causal relations that may hold among its constituents are independent parameters of a propositional attitude according to rationalist psychologies.[10]

• Suppose it's right that mental states can have logical forms to which mental processes are sensitive. The question remains *how* logical forms could determine causal powers. I'm not enough of a historian to know whether the tradition of philosophical rationalism had a consensus view on this question. But it wouldn't surprise me much to hear that it didn't, since rationalists have generally been wary of thinking of mental processes as *causal* at all.[11] It was sufficient to their purposes simply to insist, as I have also done, that the logical form of a thought isn't constituted by the causal relations among its constituents; a fortiori, it isn't constituted by the *associative* relations among its constituents.

But, of course, cognitive scientists generally *do* want to think of mental processes as causal. So if they wish to co-opt the rationalist idea that thoughts have their role in mental processes in virtue of, inter alia, their logical forms, they have to have a view about how logical form could determine causal powers. Just *saying* it does isn't good enough;

you need a mechanism. Conjoining Turing's kind of RTM to a rationalist psychology is what's supposed to provide it: For each propositional attitude that has a causal role in a mental life, there's a corresponding mental representation. Mental representations are concrete particulars, and so are allowed to cause things to happen. Also, mental representations have syntactic structures, to which mental processes are sensitive qua computations. *And the logical form of a propositional attitude supervenes on the syntax of the mental representation that corresponds to it.*[12] That is, disjunctive propositional attitudes (i.e., attitudes whose *logical* form is disjunctive) correspond to disjunctive mental representations (i.e., to mental representations whose syntactic form is disjunctive); conjunctive propositional attitudes correspond to mental representations whose *syntactic* form is conjunctive; existentially quantified propositional attitudes correspond to mental representations whose syntax is existentially quantified . . . and so on for every case in which the logical form of an attitude is invoked to explain its role in mental life.[13]

Perhaps now it starts to be clear why the notion of computation plays such a central role in how rationalist cognitive scientists think about the mind these days. A psychology (rationalist, empiricist, or whatever) needs to do more than just enunciate the laws it claims that mental processes obey. It also needs to explain *what kind of thing a mind could be* such that those laws are true of it; which is once again to say that it needs to specify a mechanism. Empiricists hold, more or less explicitly, that typical psychological laws are generalizations that specify how causal relations among mental states alter as a function of a creature's experience. Associationism provided empiricists with an explanation of why such generalizations hold, namely, that they are all special cases of the associative laws, which are themselves presumed to be innate.[14] By contrast, a rationalist psychology says that typical laws about the mind specify ways in which the logical form of a mental state determines its role in mental processes. So a rationalist is in need of a theory about how a mental process *could* be sensitive to the logical form of mental states. This theory can't, of course, be associationistic, since associative relations among mental states are supposed to hold *not* in virtue of logical form, but rather in virtue of statistical facts about (e.g.) how often they have occurred together, or how often their occurring together has lead to reinforcement, etc. Turing's notion of computation provides exactly what a rationalist cognitive scientist needs to fill this gap: It does for rationalists what the laws of association would have done for empiricists if only associationism had been true.

• Finally, it's prima facie plausible that computations in Turing's sense should somehow be what implement rationalist psychological theories. For, just as being truth preserving is the characteristic virtue of *computations* as Turing understands them, so too it is the characteristic virtue of *mental processes* as rationalists understand them. One true thought tends to lead to another in the course of cognition, and it is among the great mysteries about the mind how this could be so. Maybe this mystery can be explained on the assumption that typical inferences, insofar as they are valid in virtue of the logical structure of the thoughts involved, are implemented by computations that are driven by the syntactic structure of the corresponding mental representations.[15]

Hence a provisional merger between rationalist psychology and Turing's account of computation, of which the following are the main principles:

The Computational Theory of Mind (= a rationalist psychology implemented by syntactic processes)
i. Thoughts have their causal roles in virtue of, inter alia, their logical form.
ii. The logical form of a thought supervenes on the syntactic form of the corresponding mental representation.

iii. Mental processes (including, paradigmatically, thinking) are computations, that is, they are operations defined on the syntax of mental representations, and they are reliably truth preserving in indefinitely many cases.

The prima facie virtues of effecting this merger is that it (maybe) allows us to solve the two central problems of rationalist psychology mentioned above: "What determines the logical form of a thought?" and "How does the logical form of a thought determine its causal powers?" Answer: The logical form of a thought supervenes on the syntax of the corresponding mental representation,[16] and the logical form of a thought determines its causal powers because the syntax of a mental representation determines its computational role, as per the operations of Turing machines. So we can now (maybe) explain how thinking could be both rational and mechanical. Thinking can be rational because syntactically specified operations can be truth preserving insofar as they reconstruct relations of logical form; thinking can be mechanical because Turing machines are machines.[17]

However things eventually work out for computational nativism in cognitive science, this really is a lovely idea and we should pause a moment to admire it. Rationality is a normative property; that is, it's one that a mental process *ought* to have. This is the first time that there has ever been a remotely plausible mechanical theory of the causal powers of a normative property. The first time ever.

We now have about half of the New Synthesis in place: The cognitive mind contains whatever innate content "poverty of the stimulus" arguments require it to contain, together with an innate Turing architecture of syntactically structured mental representations and syntactically driven computational operations defined on these representations. The New Synthesis thus shares with traditional rationalism its emphasis on innate content; but it has added Turing's idea that mental architecture is computational in the proprietary syntactic sense. To round off this exposition of computational nativism, we need to explain why New Synthesis psychologists are so often proponents of the thesis that cognitive architecture is "massively modular." And why their attachment to this thesis often drives them to adaptationism in their speculations about the phylogenesis of cognition. Then we'll have the whole picture in view, and I can tell you what I think is wrong with it. In case you care.

That, however, will come later. I want to spend the rest of this chapter reflecting a little on the notion syntactic structure itself. As we've been seeing, the idea that mental representations have syntactic properties is at the heart of the nexus between rationalist psychology and the computational theory of mind. What, then, are syntactic properties?

What, Then, Are Syntactic Properties?

Well, to begin with: Syntactic properties are peculiar. On the one hand, they're among the "local" properties of representations, which is to say that they are constituted entirely by what parts a representation has and how these parts are arranged. You don't, as it were, have to look "outside" a sentence to see what its syntactic structure is, any more than you have to look outside a word to see how it is spelled. But though it's true that the syntax of a representation is a local property in that sense, it's also true that the syntax of a representation determines certain of its relations to other representations. Syntax, as it were, faces inward and outward at the same time. I want to emphasize this duality since, as we'll see in the chapter 2, both the cardinal virtues and the regrettable limitations of Turing's kind of computational psychology very largely turn on it. For the present expository purposes, I propose to talk about the syntax of sentences rather than the syntax of mental representations; but the morals apply mutatis mutandis assuming that RTM is true.

The grammatical fact that "swims" is the main verb and "John" is its subject in the sentence "John swims" is constituted entirely by facts about what the parts of that sentence are and how they are put together. But this local property of "John swims" nevertheless determines various of its relations to other English sentences: for example, that "who swims" and "does

John swim" are among the question forms of "John swims," but that *"who does John swim" is not. In consequence, if a mechanism were sensitive to the *local* syntactic structure of "John swims," it would thereby be in a position to predict such *relational* properties of the sentence as its having the question forms that it does.

Likewise for the logical form of a sentence (its logical *syntax,* as logical form is sometimes called). That a sentence has the logical form Fa is entirely a matter of the identity and arrangement of its parts; but its being of that form nevertheless constrains various of its intersentential relations. For example, if such a sentence is true, so too is the corresponding sentence of the form $\exists x(Fx)$. In consequence, a mechanism that is directly sensitive to the logical form of a sentence is thereby indirectly sensitized to certain of its entailments. It's yet another way of putting Turing's insight that local structure can encode not only grammatical relations among sentences, but inferential relations as well.[18]

Syntactic properties aren't, of course, the only ones that exhibit the kind of internal/external duality just remarked on. Here's a sort of simile, for those of you who may like such things.

Consider the famous ethology of the three-spined stickleback. All we need of it, for present purposes, is that when a male of the species is sexually active, it develops a characteristic red spot (on, approximately, its tummy) to which other sexually active male sticklebacks react with characteristic displays of territorial aggression. Now, being sexually active is a complex, largely dispositional property, the possession of which affects all sorts of relations between a stickleback and its peers. By contrast, having (or not having) a red spot on its tummy is a "local" property of sticklebacks in much the same sense that containing the word "John" is a local property of the sentence "John swims." That a stickleback has a red spot on its tummy is constituted entirely by the identity and arrangement of its parts. Here, then, is the point I want to emphasize: in consequence of the reliability of the relation between being, on the one hand, a sexually active male stickleback and, on the other hand, being a male stickleback with a red patch on its tummy, a mechanism that is able to respond (directly) to the red patch is *thereby* able to respond (indirectly) to the pattern of behavioral dispositions characteristic of a sexually active male.[19] Uncoincidentally, other male sticklebacks are notable among such mechanisms.

To be sure, this analogy between a sentence's syntax and a stickle back's tummy is imperfect. I want to stress one of the differences because it will turn out to be crucial in later chapters: Whereas the identity and arrangement of its parts is among the *essential* properties of a representation, the color of its tummy is *not* among the essential properties of a stickleback. The identity of a fish generally survives alteration of the color of its tummy, *but the identity of a sentence never survives alterations of its syntax or its logical form.* Thus, a sentence that doesn't contain "John" ipso facto can't be a token of the same type as "John is bald." Likewise a sentence that doesn't entail that someone is bald.

I think perhaps that's enough of chapter 1. We now have in place a continuation of rationalist epistemology that emphasizes inferences from poverty of the stimulus to conclusions about what cognitive contents are innate. And we have a continuation of rationalist psychology that reconstructs both the notion that mental states can have logical forms and the notion that their logical forms can be determinants of their causal powers. It does so by assuming that mental representations have syntactic structures, that the logical form of a thought supervenes on the syntactic form of the corresponding mental representation, and that mental processes are computational in a proprietary sense of "computation" that turns on the notion of a syntactically driven causal relation. So be it.

Chapter 2

Syntax and Its Discontents

Turing's idea that mental processes are computations (i.e., that they are syntactically driven), together with Chomsky's idea that poverty of the stimulus arguments set a lower bound to the information a mind must have innately, are half of the New Synthesis. The rest is the "massive modularity" thesis and the claim that cognitive architecture is a Darwinian adaptation. This chapter and the next are about how the massive modularity thesis fits in. I'm going to argue that there are some very deep problems with viewing cognition as computational, but that these problems emerge primarily in respect of mental processes that *aren't* modular. The real appeal of the massive modularity thesis is that, if it's true, we can either solve these problems, or at least contrive to deny them center stage pro tem. That's the good news. The bad news is that, since the massive modularity thesis pretty clearly *isn't* true, we're sooner or later going to have to face up to the dire inadequacies of the only remotely plausible theory of the cognitive mind that we've got so far.

So, anyhow, I shall now proceed to maintain. This chapter will be about why it probably isn't true, at least in the general case, that cognitive processes are computations. In the next chapter, we'll see how the massive modularity thesis might be supposed to avoid the objections to the generality of CTM; and why, if it doesn't, it's a mystery, not just a problem, what model of the mind cognitive science ought to try next.

Part 1, Wherein It Starts to Snow

I remarked at the end of chapter 1 that, since the syntax of a representation, mental or otherwise, is among its essential properties, the identity of an MR doesn't survive alteration of its syntax. Suppose that is so. Then Turing's idea that cognitive processes are causal only if they are syntactic is naturally read as entailing what I'll call principle E.

> *Principle E: Only essential properties of a mental representation can determine its causal role in a mental life.*

I'll use E(CTM) as a name for the doctrine you get when you do read the Computational Theory of Mind as entailing principle E. I want to emphasize that, for reasons presently to appear, insisting on principle E is arguably an overly restrictive way to interpret the idea that mental processes are syntactic. Still, I propose to pursue this reading since I think the main morals survive the relevant caveats. Suffice it for now that there are convincing reasons to think that E(CTM) could be true only if—or only insofar as—cognition is modular. If that's right, then the E(CTM) version of the computational theory of mind is captive to the massive modularity thesis. Spelling out these connections will be the main business in the next part of the discussion.

Suppose that a certain mental state has a certain role in a certain cognitive process. RTM is assumed throughout, so this cognitive process is a causal relation among mental representations. CTM is likewise assumed, so such causal relations are computations. Computations are syntactically driven by definition, so it follows that there must be some syntactic property of an MR in virtue of which the mental state has the causal role that it does. And, if we now add E(CTM), it also follows that this property of the MR must be *context invariant.* That's because the syntax of a representation is among its essential properties; and, of course, the context dependent properties of representations (or of anything else) are *not* among their essential properties. A thing's essential properties are ipso facto ones that it *always* has, *whatever* the context.[1]

Put this all together and here's what we've got:

> • Mental process are sensitive solely to the syntax of mental representations (because mental processes are computations).

- Syntactic properties of mental representations are ipso facto essential (because the syntactic properties of *any* representation are ipso facto essential).[2]
- Conclusion: Mental processes are ipso facto insensitive to context dependent properties of mental representations.

And this is where the trouble starts. For it would seem that, as a matter of fact, this conclusion isn't true; as a matter of fact, there are context-dependent determinants of the causal roles of mental representations in at least some cognitive processes. And (playing the argument in reverse now) if a determinant of the causal role of a mental representation is context dependent, then it isn't essential. *Which is contrary to E(CTM).*

Part 2: Simplicity

Simplicity is, I think, a convincing example of a context-dependent property of mental representations to which cognitive processes are responsive. It's part of rationality to prefer the simpler of two competing beliefs, ceteris paribus; and, likewise, it's part of practical intelligence to prefer the simpler of two competing plans for achieving a goal. That appeals to simplicity are ineliminable in scientific reasoning is practically axiomatic. But it would seem equally clear that comparing the relative simplicity of candidate beliefs, or of candidate plans of action, is routinely a part of reasoning in quotidian decisions about what one ought to think or do. Rube Goldberg made a living out of this. His machines are funny because they find such hard ways of solving simple problems.

We're supposing that CTM is in force, so if assessments of simplicity are to play a causal role in mental processes, the simplicity/complexity[3] of plans/theories[4] must somehow supervene on the syntax of the corresponding mental representations. Like any other causally salient intentional property of thoughts, simplicity has to correspond to a syntactic parameter of mental representations if Turing's account of cognition is right. Now, one can indeed imagine how the syntax of a mental representation might determine its simplicity in certain highly regimented cases. For example, assuming that mental representations are objects more or less like sentences, we might suppose that each of them has an *intrinsic* simplicity determined by, as it might be, the number of constituent representations it contains.[5] (The thought that the cat is on the computer would thus be simpler than the thought that the cat is asleep on the computer; which seems alright as far as it goes.) The simplicity of a whole theory might then be the sum of the intrinsic simplicities of the beliefs that belong to it, and choosing the simplest theory among the candidates would reduce to an arithmetic operation.[6] But, patently, nothing of this sort can be assumed in the general case. In the general case, the effect that adding a new thought has upon the simplicity of a theory in situ is context dependent. This is apparent if only from the consideration that the same thought that serves to complicate one theory may serve to simplify another.

Think of the simplicity of a thought as just whatever determines, for any given theory that you add it to, how much it complicates (/simplifies) that theory. Then simplicity is an *intrinsic* (i.e., *context-invariant*) property of thoughts if and only if each contributes a constant increment (/decrement) to the overall simplicity of whatever theory you conjoin it to. Pretty clearly, however, the contribution of a thought to determining the simplicity of a theory is not context invariant by this criterion. Rather, what effect adding a new belief has on the overall simplicity of one's prior epistemic commitments depends on *what one's prior epistemic commitments are.*[7] Accommodating a planetary regression or two need hardly phase your astronomy if it's of the heliocentric persuasion; but it would complicate our geocentric astronomy pretty much to extinction.

Likewise for the role of simplicity in practical reasoning. The thought that there will be no wind tomorrow significantly complicates your arrangements if you had intended to sail to Chicago, but not if your plan was to fly, drive, or walk there. But, of course, the syntax of the mental representation that expresses the thought *no wind tomorrow* is the same whichever plan you add it to. The long and short is: The complexity of a thought is not intrinsic; it depends on the context. But the syntax of a representation is one of its essential properties and so doesn't change when the representation is transported from one context to another. *So how could the simplicity of a thought supervene on its syntax?* as, please recall, CTM requires it to do.

What a thought contributes to determining the complexity of a theory is context dependent; I think I may have mentioned that. I want to stress that this is not just the truism that its contributing whatever it does to the complexity of a theory that contains it is among the *relational* properties of a thought. I'm grateful to Prof. Paolo Casalegno for suggesting the following nice way to illustrate this distinction: Say that a text is "globally odd" if it contains an odd number of words, "globally even" otherwise; and consider the contribution that the sentence "John loves Mary" makes to determining whether a text that contains it is globally odd. Query: *is this contribution context dependent?* Perhaps you're inclined to say "Sure it is; because if a given text has an odd number of words, then adding 'John loves Mary' makes the resulting text globally even; whereas, if the text has an even number of words, then adding 'John loves Mary' to it makes the resulting text globally odd."

But no. To be sure, the consideration just raised shows that its contributing what it does to the texts that you add it to is a *relational* property of "John loves Mary." But it's a *context-independent* relational property for all that. The sentence makes the same contribution whether the text you add it to is globally odd or globally even; in either case it *contributes the number of words it contains.* And, of course, containing the number of words that it does is a syntactic, hence an essential, property of a sentence, hence not context dependent. What is context dependent is not *what a sentence contributes* to determining the global oddity of a text, but rather *the result of its contributing what it contributes* in determining the global oddity of a text (see note 7). In some contexts the result of adding three words is a text that's globally odd; in other contexts it's not.

So, then, to return to the main line of the discussion: Representations contribute the same syntactic structures whatever context you add them to; but thoughts don't contribute the same degree of complexity whatever theory you add them to. So how, I asked you, could the simplicity of a thought supervene on the syntax of a mental representation? The question was rhetorical; prima facie, the answer would seem to be that it can't.

The story so far: Some of the cognitive role of a thought is plausibly determined by essential (specifically, syntactic) properties of the corresponding mental representation; the effects of the logical form of a thought on its role in demonstrative inferences is paradigmatic, and Turing's story about cognition being computational works best in this kind of case. But it seems that some determinants of the role a thought plays in mental processes may not fit this paradigm; in particular, the properties of a thought that are sensitive to *which belief systems* it's embedded in don't seem to.

Inferences in which features of an embedding theory affect the inferential-cum-causal roles of their constituent beliefs are what philosophers sometimes call "global" or "abductive" or "holistic" or "inferences to the best explanation." From now on, I'll use these terms more or less interchangeably. What they have in common, from the point of view of E(CTM), is that they are presumptive examples where the determinants of the computational role of a mental representational can shift from context to context; hence where the computational role of a mental representation is *not* determined by its individuating properties; hence where the computational role of a mental representation is not determined by its syntax. That is: what they have in common, from the point of view of E(CTM), is that they are all presumptive counterexamples.

Part 3: "Internal" and "External" Syntax

Prima facie, the line of thought I've been pursuing would seem to show that some determinants of the causal/inferential role of a thought aren't syntactic. So it would seem to show that some thinking isn't computing. *But*—this bears emphasis—*it doesn't*. Rather it shows the importance of an ambiguity that lurks in casual formulations of the idea that the causal role of a mental representation is syntactically determined. E(CTM) reads this as

claiming that the causal role of a mental representation is determined by *its* syntax; that is, by its constituent structure; that is, by
syntactic properties that the representation has in virtue of its
relations to its parts; that is, by "local" syntactic properties that
mental representations have essentially. What we've just been
seeing is that reading "syntactically determined" this way gets
E(CTM) into trouble with globality effects in mental processing.
There is, however, another, weaker way of reading "syntactic
determination" compatible with retaining the basic idea that
mental processes are computations. Consider, therefore, the what
I'll call the Minimal Computational Theory of Mind, M(CTM):

> *M(CTM): The role of a mental representation in cognitive
> processes supervenes on some syntactic facts or other.*

Notice that, strictly speaking, M(CTM) is compatible with everything that I've said so far about the importance of globality,
abduction, and the like in the life of the cognitive mind. For
example, though it seems clear that simplicity isn't an intrinsic
property of a mental representation and therefore does not
supervene on the syntax of that representation, it's still wide
open that simplicity is nonetheless a syntactic property.[8] All that
requires, according to M(CTM) is that, *given the syntax of the
representation R and of the other representations in the embedding
theory T,* the simplicity of *R* relative to *T* is fully determined. In
effect, according to this relaxed account of syntactic determination, it would be consonant with the mind's being a computer
that simplicity should supervene on *syntactic but relational*
properties of mental representations. (As do the effects of a sentence on the global oddity of texts that contain it; see above.)
Likewise, mutatis mutandis, for other prima facie global factors
in cognition.

So, assuming that M(CTM) is otherwise OK, it offers an
account of what it is for mental processes to be syntactic that's
compatible with their having global determinants. Good. On the
other hand, if there is anything wrong with M(CTM), then if
there are indeed global factors in cognition, the whole New
Synthesis story is seriously in trouble.

That is, in fact, pretty much what I take the current situation to be. I want to discuss some considerations that seem to me to make this diagnosis plausible.

The first is this: M(CTM) is good enough to save the idea that minds are "IO (input-output) equivalent" to Turing machines since, if a relation is syntactic, then some Turing machine or other can compute it.[10] But there's a clear sense in which M(CTM) isn't good enough to save the psychological plausibility of Turing's picture of how the mind works. For, by definition, which Classical computations apply to a representation is determined not just by some of its syntactic properties or other but, in particular, by its constituent structure, that is, by how the representation is constructed from its parts. Because it's that sort of syntactic fact that one has in mind, one takes it for granted that the syntax of a representation is ipso facto available to the computations for which the representation provides a domain; presumably whatever has access to X has thereby got access to its parts. But, to repeat, there are lots of syntactical facts about each representation other than the ones that comprise its constituent structure; in particular, there are lots of facts about its syntactical relations to other representations. And, on the one hand, these facts are not ipso facto accessible to computations for which the representation provides a domain; and, on the other hand, globality considerations suggest that they may well be essential to determining how the representation behaves in cognitive processes.

This last observation might look to be incompatible with the truism previously remarked upon that (in the sense of note 10) Turing machines can compute *anything* that's syntactic. If it were, then of course something serious would have gone wrong with the argument. But, on second thought, it's not. The point turns on the easily missed distinction between a claim that M(CTM) would guarantee—namely, that minds are Turing equivalent—and a claim that may well be false even if M(CTM) is true—namely, that cognitive architecture is Classical Turing architecture; that is, that the mind is interestingly like a Turing machine. Perhaps it's because these claims are easy to conflate that so many cognitive scientists take for granted that the New Synthesis *must* be true.

Suppose S is a syntactic relation between R and an embedding theory T, but one that is *not* constituted by the constituent structure of R. Then a computer can't, as it were, "see" S if all it can look at is the internal syntax of R. But that doesn't matter to the principle that any syntactic relation can be recognized by a Turing machine. That's because it is always possible to rewrite R as an expression consisting of the conjunction of R *together with the relevant parts of T*. S is then an "internal" syntactic property of the resultant longer expression, hence "visible" to computations for which the latter expression provides a domain. If, in the worst case, it should turn out that just *any* syntactic property definable over T can affect the computational role of R, then so be it; one need only assume that the shortest expression over which the computations in question are defined is the whole of T, R included.

So the claim that the cognitively relevant properties of a mental representation supervene on *its* syntax doesn't constrain the capacity of minds beyond what's already implicit in claiming that cognitively relevant properties are syntactic. But that is smallish comfort for the thesis that the architecture of cognition is Classical. For it is enormously plausible, in the typical case, that the representations over which mental processes are actually defined are *much shorter* than whole theories. Or, to put it slightly differently, it's *just got to be* possible to determine, with reasonable accuracy, the impact of adopting a new belief on one's prior epistemic commitments without having to survey those commitments in their totality. *Whole theories* can't be the units computation any more than they can be the units of confirmation, or of assertion, or of semantic evaluation.[11] The totality of one's epistemic commitments is *vastly* too large a space to have to search if all one's trying to do is figure out whether, since there are clouds, it would be wise to carry an umbrella. Indeed, the totality of one's epistemic commitments is vastly too large a space to have to search *whatever* it is that one is trying to figure out.

I regard this, by the way, as a truism not just of psychology but also of epistemology. It isn't simply that whole theories are generally too big to get one's head around—too big to think about all at once. It's also that assessments of confirmation can be, should be, and generally are called for in respect of objects much less elaborate than the totality of one's cognitive commitments. Epistemologists sometimes ignore this platitude; perhaps they argue to themselves as follows: "Duhem and Quine were right that considerations relevant to rational epistemic assessments can come from anywhere in a belief system. So it follows that whole belief systems must likewise be the *units* of confirmation. They must be, so to speak, the smallest things that properties like *being (dis)confirmed* are defined for."[12] Or, perhaps, they don't argue this to themselves, but merely slip from the premise to the conclusion without noticing. I suspect Quine himself of pretty often having done so.

But, prima facie at least, the two claims would seem to be quite different. Prima facie at least, it's one question what are the "smallest" things that "is (dis)confirmable" and the like are defined for; and it's quite a different question what considerations can decide whether a thing of that (or any other) size *is* (dis)confirmed. That (dis)confirming considerations can "come from anywhere in a theory" doesn't *begin* to be an argument that the smallest (dis)confirmed things must *be* theories. Come to think of it, bother *confirmation;* the considerations that decide whether a system of beliefs is *deductively coherent* may also "come from anywhere in the theory." It doesn't follow, and it isn't true, that the totality of one's beliefs is the smallest unit of epistemic commitment whose consistency can be affirmed or denied.

For what it's worth, I would have thought that the typical unit of confirmation is a judgment that a certain individual has a certain property. That's, as it were, the least thing that can be true, so you'd sort of expect that it's the least thing that can be confirmed. Whereas, the Duhem/Quine point about the globality of relevance has to do with something quite else: You can't decide a priori which of your beliefs bear on the assessment of which of the others because what's relevant to what depends on how things are contingently are *in the world*. Which in turn depends on how God put the world together.

But that point of epistemology, though it is deeply right-headed, is by the way. Here's where we've got to so far as the cognitive science is concerned: The effects that global features of belief systems appear to have on cognitive processes is a problem for the Classical computational account of mental architecture—that remains true *even if it's assumed that all of the global features of belief systems that have such effects are syntactic.* M(CTM) (unlike E(CTM)), allows *in principle* for abductive inferences to be computations, that is, for abductive inferences to be exhaustively syntactically driven. So the mind is Turing equivalent according to *either* E(CTM) *or* M(CTM). But as far as anybody knows, Classical psychological theorizing can exploit this loophole only at the price of a ruinous holism; that is, by assuming that the units of thought are much bigger than in fact they could possibly be. I don't really suppose that any of this comes as a surprise. I think that, deep down, everybody in cognitive science knows very well that Classical cognitive architectures have pervasive problems with modeling abductive inferences; and that the question of whether they can do so is not settled by any general considerations about Turing equivalence. The goal of the discussion so far was just to make clear the source of this worry.

We're now within hailing distance of seeing why it's plausible that Turing's kind of psychology is hostage to the massive modularity thesis, and hence of seeing how the massive modularity thesis fits into the rest of the New Synthesis story about cognition.

We'll return to all that presently. First, however, I want to develop another example of what seems to be much the same sort of point that the discussion of simplicity led us to.

Part 4: Conservatism

One is, of course, a conservative by preference. One would rather not ever change one's plans or one's beliefs, everything else being equal.[13] Likewise, if there is no alternative but to change them, one would rather do so in a way that abandons the smallest number of those in situ. Whatever may be wrong with conservatives in general, being one of the epistemic sort is constitutive of rationality. Not wanting to change your mind unless you have to is part and parcel of not wanting to have beliefs that you haven't got reasons for.

But you might expect, even at first blush, that there will be trouble reconciling the rational conservatism of belief revision with the syntactic account of mental processes as E(CTM) construes it. Here's why. At a first approximation, conservatism prefers the theory change that gives up *the fewest* prior cognitive commitments. But that can't be literally right since, surely, some beliefs count for more than others. On any remotely adequate view, conservatism requires the epistemic cost of theory change to vary as a *weighted* sum of the epistemic commitments that the change abandons. But now, it's very plausible on the face of it that this weighting is itself theory dependent; that is, that how much it would cost to abandon a belief depends on what theory it's embedded in.[14]

I assume, following Quine, that different constituents of a theory typically exhibit different degrees of *centrality*. Like most interesting notions (certainly like most notions that are epistemologically interesting) centrality is more or less comprehensively undefined. But I suppose that the intuition is clear and, by the local standards, untendentious: Theories are unequally epistemically committed to their various entailments. In the typical case, given a little patching and trimming, some of the claims that a theory endorses can be abandoned without serious damage to its main insights. By contrast, some of the others embody the very substance of the theory; give them up and there's nothing left to patch and trim. It's truistic that a rational conservatism has to be sensitive to this sort of difference, so what it must commend is holding onto as many of one's *central* epistemic commitments as one can; and, all else equal, the more central such a commitment is, the more conservatism commends one's holding onto it. This is, as I say, not particularly tendentious; and, so far, it's neutral as to whether belief revision could be a computational process as E(CTM) understands that notion. But the next step joins the issue: *Centrality is itself context sensitive.* A typical consequence of theory change is to alter the relative centrality of the beliefs that survive the change, so what seemed terribly important to hold onto prior to theory revision may be quite peripheral to the theory once it's revised; or vice versa.

There are simply zillions of examples of this; it is, as I say, a *typical* function of theories to adjudicate (if only implicitly) the relative centrality of their own commitments. So, consider the observation, reliable enough as far as it goes, that freely falling bodies generally accelerate in proportion to their weight. It's easy to suppose—indeed, physicists used to suppose—that holding onto that generalization is a do-or-die constraint on mechanics. Whatever else a mechanics ought to do, it's *at least* got to account for the observation that feathers typically fall slower than rocks. Well, feathers typically do fall slower than rocks, but we now think that that's an interaction effect, hence not a central generalization of mechanics; a fortiori not one that has to follow directly from the basic mechanical laws. To shift from a weight-centered mechanics to a mass-centered mechanics is *thereby* to demote the centrality of such generalizations about weight as happen to be preserved. The new mechanics, unlike the old one, can afford to be quite blasé about its estimates of the typical effects of weight on acceleration. By contrast, however, it's committed to defending tooth and claw its estimates of the relations between mass and effort.

Estimates of centrality are theory sensitive. It used to seem very important to get it right about the surface properties of substances; for example, because the claim that metals are ipso facto solids was supposed to be central to a good chemical taxonomy, a lot seemed to ride on mercury not being a metal. It turned out, of course, that mercury, though liquid, is a metal after all. But it also turned out that that doesn't matter, since whether a metal is a liquid depends on the ambient temperature.

The generalization that metals are typically solids (at room temperature), like the generalization that the acceleration of falling bodies is typically proportional to their weight, is true on the face of it. It's just that, in both cases, how rigorously a theory preserves these generalizations turns out not to be very important to its evaluation. It turns out, for example, that a good theory can (indeed should) perfectly well permit such generalizations to have exceptions. And, notice, it's our revised chemistry (/mechanics)—the new embedding theory itself—that shows us that our previous estimates of centrality were wrong.

Here, there, and everywhere, changing estimates of centrality are part and parcel of theory change. So estimates of which beliefs count for a lot and which ones count for a little when one is reckoning the conservatism of a theory change have to be context sensitive.[15] But the syntactic properties of representations, as E(CTM) understands that notion, *aren't* theory sensitive and *can't* change with change of context. So we're back to where the discussion of simplicity left us. It could be that centrality can be calculated over some or other syntactic relation between a belief and an embedding theory; and if so, then there's a guarantee that there's a Classical way of computing it. Here as elsewhere, assuming the truth of M(CTM) guarantees the equivalence of minds with Turing machines. However, even assuming M(CTM), the only guaranteed way of Classically computing a syntactic-but-global property is one that that takes *whole theories* as computational domains, and that's not a realistic option as a psychological model. The upshot, once again, is that the (apparent) effect of (apparently) global properties in cognition puts in jeopardy the Classical story about the architecture of cognitive processes even assuming M(CTM). And as the Classical story goes, so goes the New Synthesis.

So much for that. In the next chapter, we'll consider some of the ways in which cognitive scientists have sought to avoid facing the problems that globality, abduction, and the like raise for CTM. I'll try to convince you that the massive modularity thesis is plausibly considered as one of these; in particular, that it's a strategy for holding onto the thesis that mental processes are by and large determined by *local* properties of mental representations. In effect, it proposes to do so by denying—or, anyhow, downplaying—their globality and context sensitivity. Before we turn to that, however, I want stress that the problems that abduction raises for cognitive science aren't merely foundational; not, at least, if "merely foundational" means "merely philosophical."

On the contrary, they keep coming up, in one form or the other, all over the field. Much to the despair of the empirical inquiry.

Part 5: In Which It Is Urged That Practice Probably Proves the Pudding

It would, I suppose, be all right to just live with the tensions between the idea that mental processes are syntactic and the idea that they are global if, by and large, our cognitive science actually worked. But there's a good case to be made that much of it actually works rather badly, and that its failures trace directly to the sorts of problems that we've just been discussing: The theory that mental processes are syntactic gets it right about logical form having causal powers; but, in the course of doing so, it makes mental causation local, and that can't be true in the general case.

For example, the failure of artificial intelligence to produce successful simulations of routine commonsense cognitive competences is notorious, not to say scandalous. We still don't have the fabled machine that can make breakfast without burning down the house; or the one that can translate everyday English into everyday Italian; or the one that can summarize texts; or even the one that can learn anything much except statistical generalizations. (It's a striking peculiarity of Pinker's book in particular that he starts by remarking how hopelessly far we are from being able to build a serviceable robot, but never explains how to reconcile our inability to do so with his thesis that we know, more or less, how the cognitive mind works.)

It does seem to me that there's a pattern to the failures. Because of the context sensitivity of many parameters of quotidian abductive inferences, there is typically no way to delimit a priori the considerations that may be relevant to assessing them. In fact, there's a familiar dilemma: Reliable abduction may require, in the limit, that the whole background of epistemic commitments be somehow brought to bear in planning and belief fixation. But feasible abduction requires, in practice, that not more than a small subset of even the relevant background beliefs is actually consulted. How to make abductive inferences that are both reliable and feasible is what they call in AI the frame problem. No doubt the claim is tendentious (for further discussion see Fodor 1987), but I think it's plausibly *because* of the frame problem that our robots don't work. After all, robots are mostly computing machines. So if a lot of quotidian cognition is abductive, and if there are intrinsic tensions between abduction and computation, *why would you even expect that our robots would work?*

The failure of our AI is, in effect, the failure of the Classical Computational Theory of the Mind to perform well in practice. Failures of a theory to perform well in practice are much like failures to predict the right experimental outcomes (arguably, indeed, the latter is a special case of the former). For well-known Duhemian reasons, neither shows straight off that the theory in question is false. But neither, on the other hand, do they bode the theory in question an awful lot of good. If having such failures doesn't keep you awake at night, you're a lot more sanguine about your theories than I am about mine.

The way cognitive science was *supposed* to work was that syntactic processes implement intentional laws. If it's assumed that the syntactic properties of representations to which computations are sensitive are ipso facto local and essential, it's unsurprising that the computational story works best for inferences like $P\&Q \rightarrow P$. Inferences that simplify conjunctions are mediated by causal relations among the mental representations that express them, and the mental representation that expresses a conjunctive belief has mental representations of the conjuncts *among its syntactic constituents.* So far so good. In fact, so far *very* good. But it turns out (again unsurprisingly after all) that simplifying conjunctions is not the general case. In the general case, it appears that the properties of a representation that determine its causal-cum-inferential role, though they may be exhaustively syntactic, needn't be either local or insensitive to context. As things now stand, Classical architectures know of no reliable way to recognize such properties short of exhaustive searches of the background[16] of epistemic commitments. I think *that's* why our robots don't work.

Since all of this seems sufficiently glaring, you might think that cognitive scientists would be worried a lot about the limitations of the Classical computational theory of the mind. Speaking for myself, I'm worried half to death. In fact, it seems to me, much of the field is in deep denial; a condition to the prevalence of which the pervasive good cheer of books like Pinker's and Plotkin's offers striking testimony. As usual, the characteristic mechanism of denial is suppression. The means that the cognitive science community has devised for not thinking about the role of abductive inference in belief fixation are the matter of the next chapter.

Chapter 3

Two Ways That You Probably Can't Explain Abduction

I hope that you are at least provisionally in sympathy with the lines of argument I pursued in chapter 2; and that, in light of them, you are prepared to take it seriously that there may be a large crack in the foundations of New Synthesis cognitive architecture. If so, you might reasonably wonder why cognitive scientists don't spend more time worrying that maybe the computational theory of mental processes doesn't work for abductive inferences. As far as I can make out, there are two kinds of reasons: Psychologists who are friendly to Turing's syntactic account of computation often think that, even if they are unable to model the global determination of *ideally* rational inference, they can produce heuristic approximations good enough to account for the cognitive capacities that people actually have. And psychologists who aren't friendly to Turing's syntactic account of computation often prefer a connectionist model of cognitive architecture, which they think has no principled difficulty with holistic effects in cognition. Indeed, that's often why they prefer it.

As for me, I'm inclined to think that Chicken Little got it right. Abduction really is a terrible problem for cognitive science, one that is unlikely to be solved by any kind of theory we have heard of so far. The present chapter is about why I think neither heuristic nor connectionist approaches to abduction are promising; then, finally, we'll be in position to see where modularity and evolutionary psychology fit in.

Heuristic Solutions of the Abduction Problem

It's one thing to claim that there are global properties of belief systems to which optimally rational cognitive processes would have to attend. It's quite another thing to claim that human cognitive processes actually do attend to such properties; notoriously, human cognition makes do with rather less than optimal rationality. Perhaps, then, real cognition in real heads achieves an appearance of abductive success by local approximations to global processes; and perhaps the problem of calculating these approximations is solved heuristically, case by case. Such a proposal would be entirely compatible with the idea that cognition is computation, so long as the course of the presumed heuristic calculations is itself locally syntactically determined.

That is, in fact, the kind of suggestion that the literature often endorses when globality issues arise in discussions of what artificial intelligence calls the "frame problem." "The frame problem" is a name for one aspect of the question of how to reconcile a local notion of mental computation with the apparent holism of rational inference; in particular, with the fact that information that is relevant to the optimal solution of an abductive problem can, in principle, come from anywhere in the network of one's prior epistemic commitments. In my view, the frame problem is a lot of what makes cognition so hard to understand. Cognitive science minus the syntactic theory of computation is Hamlet without the Prince. But cognitive science minus the frame problem is Hamlet without anybody much except Polonius. (The frame problem doesn't, however, make it into the index of either Pinker's or Plotkin's book.)

So the suggestion on offer is that mental processes effect local, heuristic approximations of the global determination of abductive inference. And the prima facie objection to this suggestion is that it is circular if the inferences that are required to figure out *which* local heuristic to employ are themselves often abductive. Which there's every reason to think that they often are. If it's hard to model the impact of global considerations in *solving* a problem, it's generally equally hard to model the impact of global considerations on *deciding how* to solve a problem. This is perhaps unsurprising since deciding how to solve a problem is, of course, itself a species of problem solving.

Suppose I'm unclear whether, on balance, in the current state of the market, it would be reasonable for me to invest in potato futures.[2] Then I am likely to be equally unclear *how to decide* whether, on balance, in the current state of the market, it would be reasonable for me to invest in potato futures. And if there are grounds to suppose that abductive inferences often play a decisive role in thinking about the first sort of question, there are likely to be much the same grounds to suppose that abduction often plays a decisive role in thinking about the second. Notice, in particular, that if it is *context dependent* what role some information plays in deciding whether to buy potatoes, it is likely to be likewise context dependent what role that information plays in deciding how to decide whether to buy potatoes. That's important because context dependence and globality are two sides of the same coin. To say that a kind of inference is global is to say inter alia that there's no bound on *how much epistemic context* the rationality of drawing it may be sensitive to.

I'm told that Jones advises buying potatoes; so, for practical purposes, my question whether it is wise for me to buy potatoes is reduced to the question whether it is wise for me to do as Jones advises. But what weight I ought to assign to Jones's advice itself depends a lot on what the context is If, for example, it's *Dow* Jones, it may matter a lot that the context is financial. Deciding whether to take Jones's advice depends, in all sorts of ways, on what my prior beliefs about Jones are, just as deciding whether to buy potatoes depends, in all sorts of ways, on what my prior beliefs about the market are. There is nothing to indicate that the determinants of reliable cognitive processing become decreasingly global, which is to say decreasingly context dependent, as one goes up this hierarchy of decision making.

I now propose a brief methodological digression, the point of which will become apparent in a paragraph or so. I hope.

There are really two kinds of computational psychological explanation, the ones that are computational strictu dictu, and the architectural ones. Roughly, what I'm calling "computational explanations strictu dictu" might be thought of as exhibiting derivations—causal sequences of mental representations—of which the last line is typically a specification of the behavior to be explained.[3] Whereas, by contrast, what I'm calling "architectural" explanations answer questions about how—by what causal process—the mind gets from one line in such a derivation to the next. The point of present concern is that architectural explanations are indispensable to any theory that endorses explanations that are strictu dictu computational. The relevant considerations are of much the sort that arose in Achilles' famous discussion with the tortoise. Since they are familiar, and pretty much common ground among cognitive scientists, I won't belabor them here. Suffice it for an example that it is likely often to be important to the proper operation of a Classical computer that it get from the premises to the conclusion of a modus ponens argument. The reason it is able to do so, the tortoise to the contrary notwithstanding, is basically this: Given a derivation which includes formulas of the form A and $A \rightarrow B$, the detachment of B is effected automatically by an architectural process (in particular, it requires no further premises or derivations) if A and B are primitive expressions.

So, now the point of the digression: If there are to be heuristic solutions of problems about what to do or believe, there must be something that decides which heuristics to use in solving them. And, so long as the general Turing framework is assumed and the postulation of bona fide global cognitive processes is not an option, there are only two possibilities. Either such higher-order decisions are effected computationally (i.e., locally), or noncomputationally and automatically (i.e., as a causal consequence of the way that token mental representations interact with the cognitive architecture). These two are the only options consonant with assuming that computations are ipso facto local and that the distinction "computational/architectural" is exhaustive.

Now, it's clear enough why, on the present assumptions, the first option won't do: We're supposing that bona fide abductive inference is often involved in the choice of a problem-solving heuristic; and bona fide abductive inferences are nonlocal, hence noncomputational, by definition. But the second option is still open, and you might reasonably want to know what's wrong with it. The most we've got so far is a reason to doubt that the Classical story can offer a "strictu dictu computational" explanation of the role of abduction in cognitive processes. But why shouldn't it tell a story that accommodates global inference *in the architecture?*

Well, because in Classical models, the *architectural* processes are all local, just like the computations. That is, no such process is irreducibly sensitive to global properties of belief systems. Rather, they all are (or reduce to) operations defined over symbols that belong to the *primitive* vocabulary of the language that the machine computes in (they are operations like, e.g., writing a primitive symbol, deleting a primitive symbol, and the like). The effect, to repeat, is that in Classical machines, the basic architectural processes as well as the basic computational ones are local; they respond (only) to the identity and arrangement of primitive representations.

In contrast, of course, the problem about globality is that there appear to be mental process—architectural or computational or both, who knows?—that respond to (irreducibly) nonlocal properties of belief systems; and we don't understand how such processes work. We don't understand how either a psychologically plausible computational process or a psychologically plausible architectural process could be rational (say, in the sense of reliably-truth preserving) and not reducible to local operations. In particular, precisely the point I've been laboring to make is that Turing doesn't even *purport* to answer this question: he was into showing how processes that are either computational or architectural (or both) can be rational if they *do* reduce to local operations. That's what makes Turing's sort of psychology Classical, and vice versa.

It bears emphasis that although the Classical account provides no reconstruction of the notion of a global architectural process, there is nothing in the least far-fetched about the thought that there might be some.[4] There are patently indefinitely many properties of a complex mental representation (or of anything else) that do not reduce to (or even supervene on) the identity and arrangement of its primitive parts. Being the first token of its mental representation type since Christmas would be an example. So, if a certain operation applies to a mental representation depending on whether it's the first representation of its type since Christmas then, strictly speaking, *that operation isn't compu-tational or architectural* insofar as the Classical theory reconstructs these notions. (The example is by no means fantastic; UK readers are invited to consider the pervasive and deleterious cognitive consequences of the Boxing Day blues.)

So why don't Classical theorists (or anybody else) worry about the possibility of mental processes that are sensitive to time elapsed since Christmas? The answer is patent: although they wouldn't, strictly speaking, be computational or architectural in the Classical sense, it's perfectly clear how they could nonetheless be entirely mechanical. All you'd need to model them is a clock. Well, the problems about globality would likewise go away if only we had a story to tell about how *they* could be mechanical without being either "computational" or "architectural" (in, to repeat, the proprietary, local sense of those notions that Classical theory reconstructs). But we don't. So they don't.

Abduction and Connectionism

The immediately preceding discussion ran on two assumptions: *First,* that the appearance of global effects in cognition needs to be taken seriously. I'm quite prepared to admit that it may yet turn out that all cognitive processes reduce to local ones, and hence that abductive inference is after all achieved in some way that Classical computational psychology can accommodate. But nothing of the sort is currently on offer, and I wouldn't advise your holding your breath. *Second,* that Turing was right about cognitive processes being computations in the proprietary sense of principle E, chapter 2. It was adhering to the Turing story that led us to take for granted that all cognitive processes reduce to local ones. And it was that, in turn, that made bona fide abduc-tion (as opposed to its heuristic approximation) begin to look impossible.

So, then, none of the arguments so far should worry you at all if you are able to believe that the appearance of global effects in cognitive processing does not need to be taken seriously. Alternatively, if you find that hard to believe, you might want to consider giving up on the Turing story as a general account of how the cognitive mind works. Indeed, I am inclined to think that, sooner or later, we will *all* have to give up on the Turing story as a general account of how the mind works, and hence, a fortiori, that we will have to give up on the generality of New Synthesis cognitive science. Considerations of the kind discussed in chapter 1, about the causal consequences of logical form, suggest that cognitive processes consist inter alia of local syntactic operations on mental representations. But considerations about the globality of some kinds of mental processes suggest that cognition can't consist *just* of syntactic operations on mental representations. So be it; thus far has The World Spirit progressed.

On the other hand, taken in and of itself, the suggestion that the explanation of abduction lies in the right choice of a cognitive architecture is simply empty. All that cognitive architectures have in common *as such* is that their operations are by assumption mechanical. Likewise, all that the alternatives to Classical architectures have in common as such is that their operations are by assumption mechanical but not Classical. The substantive problem is to understand, even to a first approximation, *what sort* of architecture cognitive science ought to switch to insofar as the goal is to accommodate abduction. As far as I know, however, nobody has the slightest idea.

In particular, the standard current alternative to Turing architecture, namely, connectionist networks, is simply hopeless. Here, as so often elsewhere, networks contrive to make the worst of both worlds. They notoriously can't do what Turing architectures can, namely, provide a plausible account of the causal consequences of logical form. But they also can't do what Turing architectures can't, namely, provide a plausible account of abductive inference. It must be the sheer magnitude of their incompetence that makes them so popular.

The claim that network architectures have principled problems about abduction—indeed, the same principled problems about abduction that Turing architectures have, though for slightly different reasons—may strike you as not plausible. After all, abduction is about globality-cum-context-sensitivity, and much of the advertising for networks is about how very global and context sensitive they are. That line of thought is natural, but quite wrong; the rest of this chapter will try to make clear what's wrong with it. I commence with a short account of what networks are. Since you probably already know what I'm about to tell you, it will be very short indeed. (There are many much more comprehensive expositions in the literature; see, e.g., chapter 2 of Elman et al. 1995.)

What makes a machine a network is that it has a computational architecture that differs, in various ways, from the classical architecture of Turing machines (or of von Neumann machines, or desktop computers). One of the differences is that networks don't exhibit the distinction between program and memory that is characteristic of the more familiar devices. Rather, both the current computational proclivities of a network and the residual effects of its computational history are determined by varying the strength of connectivity among a (typically large) number of simple, switchlike elements. At a given time, each of these elements is in one of two output states: quiescent (=0) or firing (=1). If you specify the firing state of each of the elements at that instant, together with the strength of each of the node-to-node connections, you thereby determine which elements will fire next, and what the subsequent connection strengths will be. You won't go far wrong if you think of the elements as analogous to Ideas (in, say, Hume's sense) and the strength of the connectivity between elements as analogous to the degree to which the corresponding Ideas are associated. For an element to fire at t is for the corresponding Idea to be entertained at t; the probability that an Idea will be entertained at t is a function of (inter alia)[5] the strength of its connections to whatever Ideas were entertained the instant before; and the strength of the association between Ideas is a function of (inter alia) the frequency of which entertaining the one is the (causal) consequence of having entertained the other.[6]

Connectionist models compute in parallel by sending waves of activation through networks of such elements. Activation is initiated by exciting the "input nodes" (by sensory stimulations if you're talking Hume). How much of this activation goes where at time t depends on the network's history of activations prior to *t*, which is in turn encoded by the strengths of the various node-to-node connections at *t*. So the long and short is: What you are thinking about at *t* is a function of your sensations together with the strength of your associations at *t*. The psychologist's job is to make this function explicit by articulating the laws that determine the strengths of the associative relations. That's what's so nice about empiricist cognitive science: You can drop out for a couple of centuries and not miss a thing.

So much, then, for what kinds of devices networks are. In what sense can "globality" be claimed for them, and in what sense not? And what has any of this got to do with abductive inference and the like? I want to start with a point from chapter 2. In Classical, Turing-style cognitive science, the causal powers of a mental representation (the role it plays in cognitive processes) are determined by its local syntax, which is in turn determined entirely by the identity and arrangement of its primitive parts. Local syntactic properties are essential in the sense that representations that are locally syntactically distinct are ipso facto type distinct. Now compare the individuation and causal powers of the nodes in networks. Nodes are simples; by definition; they have no parts. A fortiori, they have no syntactic parts. A fortiori, the type identity of nodes is not determined by the identity and arrangement of their constituents.

So what is it about a node token that determines which node type it belongs to? Answer: its position in its network, where its network is the totality of the nodes to which it is (directly or indirectly) connected. Two nodes in different networks (e.g., in networks that don't have the same number of nodes; or in networks that have the same number of nodes, but different connectivity) ipso facto belong to different node types; just as, in Classical architectures, two expressions that differ in their constituency ipso facto belong to different expression types. Likewise, since nodes in different networks, or at different positions in the same network, are ipso facto different types of nodes, it follows that its position in its network is among a node's *essential* features. Just as a Classical representation can't change its local syntax, so a node can't change what network it's in or where it is in that network.

It's because the essential properties of a node all involve its relations to the network it's embedded in that nodes *can't* be "transported" from one network to another; just as it's because the essential properties of a Classical representation all involve its relation to its parts that it *can* be transported from theory to theory. Likewise, and for the same reason, whereas a node of a given type can appear only once in the network that embeds it, a given Classical representation can be repeated indefinitely in a given text. In short, there really is something global about networks, namely, the individuation conditions of the nodes that belong to them. Equivalently: the "smallest" unit of connectionist representation for which a type/token relation is definable is a whole network. In consequence, connectionists have a notorious problem reconciling the way that they individuate nodes with patent truths about the productivity, systematicity, and compositionality of typical cognitive systems: On one hand, all these phenomena appear to depend on complex mental representations' being constructed from recurrent parts in different arrangements; but on the other hand, network architectures haven't any way to say that representations *can* have recurrent parts, for example, that "John loves Mary" and "Mary loves John" do.[8]

These sorts of problems about connectionist architectures are familiar from the cognitive science literature. But there is a further charge as well; one that's closer to our present concerns. Networks have much the same trouble with abductive inference that Classical architectures do (though, to repeat, for a slightly different reason). Consider, for example, the worry about how Classical models are to reconstruct the effects of the "centrality" of representations on their cognitive roles. Let me remind you what the worry was: Prima facie, the centrality of a representation changes as you go from one belief system to the next, but the local syntax of the representation doesn't; local syntax is context independent. So, assuming that cognitive processes are sensitive exclusively to local syntax, how does Classical psychology recover the fact that the same belief may have different centrality in different theories? Nobody knows. Well, the present point is that if Classical models aren't able to answer this question, networks aren't even able to *ask* it. For, to repeat, the type-individuation conditions that network architectures afford are incompatible with a node's being identified transtheoretically.[9] And, if it can't even be true that the same representation occurs in more than one theory, then of course it can't be true that a representation survives the transition from one theory to the next.

Unsurprisingly, if an architecture can't do centrality, it can't do relevance either. Suppose a network is so wired that information at node 3 is accessible to node 1 only via changes of state of node 2. Then nothing that subsequently happens to the network can alter that arrangement. The most that can happen is that the flow of information along the route from node 1 to node 3 is facilitated (or impeded) as experience alters the strength of the connections in accordance with the presumed associative laws. This is to say, in effect, that a network can't change its mind about whether what's represented at one node is directly relevant to what's represented at another node (or, if the relevance is indirect, about how indirect it is). That estimates of relevance are, in this sense, unlabile in connectionist systems is, to repeat, a defining property of the architecture; it follows from the defining condition for node types. All of which seems to fly in the face of the fact that I harped on in chapter 2: Changing estimates of relevance appears to be a routine consequence of quotidian changes of contingent beliefs.[10]

Please, please do not reply to the foregoing that a connectionist, even if he can't have a transtheoretic notion of node identity, might make do with a transtheoretic notion of node (or network) *similarity*. There isn't any such notion, and there isn't any prospect of one that avoids patent circularity. For, presumably what would make two nodes transtheoretically similar is that they share some (but not all) of their connectivity; that is, that some (but not all) of the nodes they are connected to are nodes of the same type. *But there isn't a transtheoretic notion of type identity for nodes;* that's the very problem I've been raising. There's a general moral, one that Lepore and I emphasized in our book *Holism* (1992; see also Fodor and Lepore 1999): In all the cases we've heard of, a robust notion of similarity presupposes a correspondingly robust notion of identity. There is no reason in the world to suppose that network architectures are exempt from this.

So, one might fairly summarize the connectionist's situation as follows: His architecture gives him holism, to be sure. But he gets it just where he doesn't want it, namely, in the individuation of mental representations. In consequence, he can't make sense of the conservatism of theory change or, indeed, of any other such transtheoretical properties of mental processes. And, having abandoned the idea that mental states have constituent structure, he is also unable to make sense of the causal consequences of logical form. Connectionism is thus able to understand even less about the cognitive mind than New Synthesis Classicism does. (If you want to understand even less about the cognitive mind than Connectionism does, I suppose you will have to become a behaviorist.)[11]

So now what? I can think of several research strategies that one might consider in this impasse.

> (i) Do nothing about abduction; wait till someone has a good idea.

This is, no doubt, the rational strategy; quite possibly the only one that will work. But it ignores the exigencies of the tenure system and is therefore impractical.

> (ii) Argue that the apparent nonlocality of quotidian cognitive processes is somehow an illusion; everything's perfectly alright, and the syntactic view of computation will be vindicated in the fullness of time.

> (ii.a) (A variant.) Scientific inference may really sometimes be abductive; but then, science is social, whereas quotidian cognition, of the kind psychologists care about, is carried out in single heads. Psychology isn't, after all, the philosophy of science writ small.

As to (ii): As a philosopher friend of mine likes to say at this sort of juncture: "Believe it if you can." I can't.

As to (ii.a): It strikes me as wildly implausible that the structure of human cognition changed radically a few hundred years ago. (For that matter, it strikes me as wildly implausible that the structure of human cognition has *ever* changed radically.) In any case, this a book for nativists.

> *(iii) Admit that there really is a problem, but cling to the hope that heuristic approximations will eventually nibble it down to size.*

This is, I suppose, de facto the research strategy that Classical cognitive science has pursued with respect to the globality issues. The results, so far, strike me as not promising.

> *(iv) For the time, concentrate one's research efforts in those areas of cognitive processing where the effects of globality are minimal; minimal enough, indeed, so that they can be ignored salve (not just reasonable adequacy but) a reasonable degree of scientific insight.*

I do urge you to consider the fourth option seriously (which, of course, is not the same as urging that you adopt it). For one thing, it is compatible with the simultaneous and rigorous pursuit of option (i). For another thing, it has the effect of connecting issues about abduction with issues about whether cognition is modular. The Patient Reader may recall a question that's been on our agenda all along, which is: "How does the New Synthesis commitment to modularity connect with the New Synthesis commitment to a computational theory of mind?" We are now, at long last, ready to turn to that. I expect it's time for a New Chapter.

Chapter 4

How Many Modules Would You Say There Are?

I think I'll start this chapter with some of its main conclusions:

It was the burden of chapters 2 and 3 that globality is, perhaps irremovably, a thorn in the flesh of the theory that cognitive processes are Classical computations. However, on at least some views of cognition, the architecture of the mind is modular; and, on at least one understanding of what a module is, modular processes are ipso facto local. Or, anyhow, relatively local. If that's right, there are morals that might be derived, depending on *how much* of cognition is modular:

> i. If none of it is, skip this chapter and the next.
> ii. If only part of it is, then a reasonable research strategy might concentrate on that part until somebody has a good idea about abduction.
> iii. If most or all of it is, then something is badly wrong with my claim that abduction is a deep and pervasive problem for cognitive science. In which case, Pinker and Plotkin are probably right about the prospects for New Synthesis Psychology being very good, and I have been wasting your time. (Mine too, come to think of it.)

Call the idea that most or all of cognition is modular the "massive modularity" thesis (MM). Then the upshot is that the likelihood that New Synthesis Psychology will turn out to be a reasonably general theory of the cognitive mind is hostage to MM. But (so I'll argue) there are good reasons to doubt that MM is true: Taken literally, it verges on incoherence. Taken liberally, it lacks empirical plausibility. If this picture of our general situation is more or less right, then there is a lot we don't know about how the cognitive mind works.

So much for the conclusions at which we'll arrive. We'll get to them in stages.

Stage 1: What's a Module?[1]

A lot of quite different things get called "the modularity thesis" in the cognitive science literature. Many of them are themselves congeries of relatively independent doctrines, so you can, if you like, make up new modularity theses by mixing and matching from the ones already in the field. I see no need to legislate usage even if it were possible to do so. But, clearly, what one ought to say about the relation between modularity and abduction, or about whether the mind is massively modular, depends on what one takes a module to be. So let's start with that.

I think there are basically two kinds of cognitive architectures that people have in mind as modular, each with a number of sub-options. The big division is between notions of modularity that imply "informational encapsulation" (about which, see below) and notions of modularity that don't. Only the first sort are germane to our concerns, but, for orientation, I'll start with a little about the second.

Modularity without Encapsulation[2]

1. There is a usage according to which anything that is or purports to be a *functionally individuated* cognitive mechanism—anything that would have its proprietary box in a psychologist's information flow diagram—thereby counts as a module.[3] If you assume that some sort of "homuncular functionalism" (see, e.g., Fodor 1968; Cummins 1983) is the appropriate metaphysics for psychological explanations, then each of the several homunculi that jointly constitute a mind counts as a module. Probably everybody who thinks that mental states have any sort of structure that's specifiable in functional terms qualifies as a modularity theorist in this diluted sense. I guess that leaves out only behaviorists and Gibsonians (who think there aren't any mental states), connectionists (who think that yes there are, but they don't have

any structure), and reductionists (who think that yes they do, but their individuation is neurological). In contrast to all of these, I shall simply take it for granted that cognition is typically the interaction of many functionally individuated parts, and use "modularity thesis" as the name of something more tendentious.

2. There is a usage proprietary to Noam Chomsky (e.g., 1980) in which a module is simply a body of innate knowledge (or, by preference, a body of "innately cognized" propositional contents). For reasons of the sort we discussed in chapter 1, modules in this sense are noncommittal with respect to just about all issues about the architecture of mental *processes*. Much of the terminological confusion about modules in the cognitive science literature derives from an unhelpful policy adopted by Fodor (1983), where Chomsky's term for innate databases is borrowed to refer to mechanisms of informationally encapsulated cognitive processing. The putative connection between Chomsky's kind of modules and Fodor's kind, according to MOM, is that bodies of innate knowledge are typically processed by encapsulated cognitive mechanisms; and, vice versa, that encapsulated cognitive mechanisms are typically dedicated to the processing of innate databases (e.g., to the integration of innate information with sensory inputs early in the course of perceptual analysis). The idea that this is the typical relation between Chomsky's sort of modules and my sort continues to strike me as plausible.

Anyhow, for better or worse, the neologistic usage according to which modules are informationally encapsulated mechanisms of cognitive processing is now common in the field. Since, as we're about to see, issues about encapsulation and issues about abduction are arguably two sides of the same coin, I want to emphasize that Chomskian modules are largely neutral about both. If abductive inference is widely characteristic of cognitive processes, then it is presumably likewise widely characteristic of such cognitive processes as interact with Chomskian modules. If not, then presumably not. Either way, as I understand the geography, the argument between nativists and empiricists that Chomsky revived is orthogonal to the argument over whether, or to what extent, mental processes are encapsulated.[4] Insofar as the former issue comes up in the present discussion, I'll usually assume that more or less strict nativism is true about encapsulated cognition. But alternative views of modularity can be imagined. For a kind of theory on which encapsulation is primarily an outcome of ontogenetic rather than phylogenetic processes, see Karmiloff-Smith 1992; for an unsympathetic assessment of that kind of theory, see Fodor (1998a; chapters 11 and 12).

So, then: A module *sans phrase* is an informationally encapsulated cognitive mechanism, and is presumed innate barring explicit notice to the contrary. A "Chomskian module" is an innate database.[5] Functionally individuated cognitive mechanisms as such will be referred to as functionally individuated cognitive mechanisms, never as modules.

Domain specificity
It's often said that what makes something a module is that it's "domain specific." There's point to this, I think, but it needs to be handled with care. The next page or two will therefore be devoted to sorting out what "domain specificity" means in theories that use it to say what "modularity" means. I'm afraid that this is going to seem a bit scholastic. But it will help, when we get to the main issues, if we're all agreed on what we're talking about.

If your notion of a module is Chomskian, then there is a merely truistic reading of the idea that modules are domain specific. For Chomskian modules are bodies of information (see above), and information is ipso facto specific to the domain that it is information about. The information that cows have horns is specific to cows. The information that everything that exists is spatially extended is specific to everything that exists; the information that cats scratch is specific to cats; and so on. This notion of the domain specificity of information is, patently, of no use to anybody. I mention it simply to get it out of the way.

Here's another sense in which information per se might be said to be (or not to be) domain specific: Information about some properties of things is more general than information about other properties of things in that there are some properties that lots of things have, and others that not many do, and still others that none do. "Has horns," for example, is true of fewer things than "is spatially extended," so there's a (perhaps slightly tortured) sense in which information about horns is more domain specific than information about spatial extension. If one chooses to talk this way, then the "domain" of a body of information is whatever it is true of, and a "domain-specific" body of information is one that holds only in a relatively small domain. Presumably, when Chomsky talks of the language module as domain specific, it's this sort of thing that he has in mind. The idea is that the properties of natural languages are more or less sui generis; in particular, sentences, structural descriptions, and the like are *atypical* products of human mentation. The domain specificity of the putative innate theory of language that Chomsky calls "General Linguistic Theory" is thus of a kind with the domain specificity of the biology of the duck-billed platypus. In both cases, it consists of there not being many things of that sort around.

I have no objection to this way of talking. But it does bear emphasis that, so construed, domain specificity is neutral with respect to issues about abduction and the like. Information that's true just of platypuses holds, ipso facto, in a very limited domain. But that it does so says nothing about how such information is learned; or about the character of the mental processes that transpire when one reasons about the (or a) platypus. Likewise, mutatis mutandis, for the information specified by GLT. In contrast, what I'm trying to converge on is a notion of modularity-cum-domain-specificity that does connect with issues of that kind.

Implicit in the conversation so far is a distinction between modularity theories according to which domain specificity is primarily a property of *information* and modularity theories according to which it isn't. The latter kind generally take domain specificity to be a property of *processes*. I think this is a step in a useful direction; but the connection between modularity and domain specificity remains less than obvious even if you are prepared to take it. The problem, once again, is to avoid the trivialization of domain specificity claims. Just as information is ipso facto specific to whatever it's about, so processes are ipso facto specific to whatever they apply to. That's just truistic, so it can't be what the modularity of cognitive processes consists in if the claim that they are modular is to be of any empirical interest.[6]

Consider, for example: "Is modus ponens (MP) a domain-specific kind of inference?"

> • Well, yes. After all, MP applies only to arguments with premises of the form P; $P \rightarrow Q$. The number of arguments that *aren't* of that form is enormous, even as compared with the number of animals that aren't platypuses.

But, on the other hand:

> • Well, no. Since MP abstracts entirely from the content of the premises it applies to, inferences in quite different domains (physics and literary theory, as it might be) may none the less both be instances of MP.

Which of these is the right thing to say? Presumably neither. The notion of domain specificity, at least insofar as it's supposed to connect with the notion of modularity, doesn't apply to *processes* per se, any more than it applies to *information* per se. *Rather, it applies to the way that information and process interact.* As we are now about to see.

If you think of MP the way that logicians do, then inferences of that form are indistinguishable at the level of representation at which their validity is assessed. In particular, they're all valid *qua* inference of the form: $(P, P \rightarrow Q)$ *hence Q*. This is just another way to say that whether an inference is an instance of MP is independent of the inferential domain (i.e., it's independent of the nonlogical content of the premises and conclusions). It would thus be a reasonable guess that if an inference-making mechanism has access to MP at all, it should be about equally good at assessing arguments of that form *whatever domain they are drawn from.*[7] For example, it should be about as good at, say (i):

(i) *If 2 is prime then it's odd; 2 is prime; so 2 is odd*

as it is at, say, (ii):

> (ii) *If a liquid contains water it's a poison; orangeade contains water; so orangeade is a poison.*

It is an empirical issue that is hotly debated among cognitive psychologists whether the mechanisms of quotidian cognition are typically indifferent to content in the ways that MP is in its standard formulation. Some psychologists think that such proneness to domain-neutral forms of inference as we may actually have is an artifact of education; logic is (just) something that one learns in school. ("I haven't used modus ponens for weeks," one connectionist is reported to have said in the course of a lecture on logic and thought.) That, no doubt, is an extreme of gnosticism. But, clearly, one can imagine a mechanism that assesses inferences by reference to a rule of modus ponens formulated *with less than complete generality,* and this may bring us closer to a notion of domain specificity that is useful for saying what a module is. Perhaps, for example, the principle appealed to in the assessment of (i) is something like (iii).

> (iii) *2 is F; if 2 is F then 2 is G; so 2 is G*

Since (iii) is valid, and since (i) is an instance of (iii) every bit as much as it is an instance of MP ("instance of" is transitive), (iii) will do just as well as MP to use in assessing (i). The present point is that, for a device that works this way, there is an intrinsic interaction of inferential domain with the availability of MP; in effect, it has access to MP, but only for purposes of reasoning about the number 2.[8] That being supposed, the fact that the device is reliable in its assessments of inferences like (i) would be *no reason at all* to expect it to be reliable in its assessments of inferences like (ii). I will say that a cognitive process is "domain specific" whenever its availability depends on problem domains in this sort of way; hence the remark with which this part of the discussion opened, that "domain specific," in the sense of the term I'm concerned with, applies neither to information nor to processes, but rather to the way that the two of them interact.[9]

This brings us to informational encapsulation; which will in turn bring us to what a module is; which will in turn bring the chapter to the end of Stage 1.

Informational encapsulation
Imagine that the following kind of situation arises in the mental life of an organism: A certain piece of information (and/or a certain rule of inference) is, in principle, relevant to the creature's success both in tasks drawn from domain *A* and in tasks drawn from domain *B*. But though the creature reliably uses the information to perform one kind of task, it seems unable to do so when it is required to perform tasks of the other kind; and this asymmetry persists when extraneous (e.g., attentional or motivational) variables are controlled. So, presumably (some of) the cognitive mechanisms that the creature brings to bear in performing the task are domain specific in the sense just sketched. Just to have a term of art, let's say that one of them is *encapsulated* with respect to information that is accessible to the other. We saw one of the ways in which this might come about when we imagined a mind that has MP in a less than fully generally form, and is thus good at assessing inferences like (i) but bad at assessing inferences like (ii).[10]

There are other ways in which this sort of situation might arise. One can imagine a kind of mind that represents its principles of inference with full generality, but can only call upon them when it is reasoning about numbers, or only when it's navigating by dead reckoning (or only when it's thinking about sheep, for that matter). That might be because it has different mechanisms for each of the different content domains, and there are restrictions on how information can flow from any one of these mechanisms to any of the others. For example, the bit of the logic module that knows about modus ponens might be connected to the bit of the navigation module that knows about dead reckoning, but not to the bit of the numerical module that knows about prime numbers. In which case, the creature might be able to do inferences of the form MP when it is thinking about where it is, but not when it is thinking about primes. The difference between this kind of arrangement and the one we imagined just above is that here it's the *distribution,* rather than the *formulation* of the information that makes its applicability domain specific. What both kinds of arrangement have in common is that, for one reason or other, the information that is available to perform a task depends on which task it is; and the constraints in virtue of which this is so are "architectural" (they're not effects of resource limitations, and they're not sensitive to the creature's preferences).[11]

I can now, at last, say what I'm taking a module to be. Imagine a computational system with a proprietary (e.g., Chomskian) database. Imagine that this device operates to map its characteristic inputs onto its characteristic outputs (in effect, to compute a function from the one to the other) and that, in the course of doing so, its informational resources are restricted to what its proprietary database contains. That is, the system is "encapsulated" with respect to information that is *not* in its database. (This might be for either, or both, of the kinds of reasons considered above: Its operations are defined with less than full generality or its informational exchanges with other processing mechanisms are constrained.) That's what I mean by a module. In my view, it's informational encapsulation, however achieved, that's at the heart of modularity.[12]

It should already be clear why modularity, so construed, might be of interest to anybody who is worried about abduction; for example, to anybody who is worried that the globality of cognitive processes comports badly with the theory that they are Classical computations. In a nutshell: Modules are informationally encapsulated by definition. And, likewise by definition, the more encapsulated the informational resources to which a computational mechanism has access, the less the character of its operations is sensitive to global properties of belief systems. Thus, to the extent that the information accessible to a device is architecturally constrained to a proprietary database, it won't have a frame problem and it won't have a relevance problem (assuming that these are different); not, at least, if the database is small enough to permit approximations to exhaustive searches. Frame problems and relevance problems are about how deeply, in the course of cognitive processing, a mind should examine its background of epistemic commitments. A modular problem-solving mechanism doesn't have to worry about that sort of thing because, in point of architecture, only what's in its database can be in the frame. This means, in particular, that to the extent that a system is modular, it doesn't have to treat framing as a *computational* problem. (Compare the discussion of heuristic approaches to abduction in chapter 3.) Likewise for centrality, simplicity, and the other skeletons in Turing's closet. To a first approximation, nothing affects the course of computations of an encapsulated processor except what gets inside the capsule; and the more the processor is encapsulated, the less information that is. The extreme case is, I suppose, the reflex; it's encapsulated with respect to all information except what's in the current input. So it operates entirely without computing, and goes off automatically or not at all.

Here is the moral so far. Classical computations are sensitive, at most, to the local context; and so too are the computations that modular mechanisms perform. It is thus unsurprising that modular cognition is the kind of processing of which the Classical computational story is the most likely to be true.

Stage 2: Massive Modularity

Suppose the cognitive mind is largely modular. This means that there is a more or less encapsulated processor for each kind of problem that it can solve; and, in particular, that there is nothing in the mind that can ask questions about which solution to a problem is "best overall," that is, best in light of the totality of a creature's beliefs and utilities. If that's right, then, as I remarked above, there must be something badly wrong with my claim that the New Synthesis (and, in particular, the Classical account of cognitive processes) is suffering from terminal abduction. Well, if so, so be it; I've been wrong before. In the discussion that follows, I therefore propose to waive the worries about globality that I've been raising and consider the massive modularity thesis on its own terms. I'm going to argue that there's no a priori reason why MM *should* be true; that the most extreme versions of MM simply *can't* be true; and that there is, in fact, no convincing evidence that anything of the sort *is* true. In sum, no cheers for MM.

A priori arguments for massive modularity

It's sometimes claimed (especially, of late, by Tooby and Cosmides) that there are very general, adaptationist considerations that, a priori and sight unseen, militate in favor of massively modular cognitive architectures over domain-general architectures, or "mixed" ones that acknowledge computational mechanisms of both kinds. Actually, I find it hard to believe that there could be such arguments. For, clearly, any architecture must be a choice among virtues not all of which can be simultaneously maximized: Speed vs. accuracy, memory space vs. computing space, "depth" of computation vs. "spread" of computation, and so on and on. There are, of course, indefinitely many imaginable mixtures. Different ways of organizing cognition play such trade-offs differently, and presumably the relative fitness of the resulting cognitive system must depend on lots on details of its relation to the local ecology. If so, it's hard to imagine that any given kind of architecture could plausibly be shown to be, as it were, fittest come what may; which is, after all, what a seriously a priori argument for MM would have to do.

Still, I want to take a quick look at some arguments of that sort that have recently been proposed, because, remarkably, a number of cognitive scientists have apparently found them persuasive.

In their 1994 paper, Cosmides and Tooby make the following remarkably strong claim (their italics): *"[It] is in principle impossible for a human psychology that contained nothing but domain-general mechanisms to have evolved, because such a system cannot consistently behave adaptively: It cannot solve the problems that must have been solved in ancestral environments for us to be here today"* (p. 90). Now, I'm a modularity fan myself; and I don't think it's likely, what with one thing and another, that the human mind consists of "nothing but domain general mechanisms." But "impossible"? "in principle"? Golly!

In fact, according to Cosmides and Tooby there are *three* reasons why it's "impossible in principle" that the human mind consists of nothing but domain-general mechanisms. I must admit that I don't find them moving, severally or together.

Reason 1. "The definition of error is domain-dependent. . . . But there is no domain-independent criterion of [cognitive] success or failure that is correlated with fitness. This is because what counts as fit behavior differs markedly from domain to domain. For example, suppose our hypothetical domain-general learning mechanism guiding an ancestral hunter-gatherer somehow inferred that sexual intercourse is a necessary condition for producing offspring. Should the individual, then, have sex at every opportunity?" (p. 91). I've quoted relatively at length because, in light of the example, I'm less than certain exactly how the argument is supposed to go. It sounds like what's wrong with the putative ancestor is his not having noticed that with sex, as with so much else in life, enough is enough. If, however, you're prepared to accept that a domain-general mechanism could learn that sexual intercourse is a necessary condition for producing offspring, it's unclear to me why the same domain general mechanism mightn't be able to learn how much is likely to suffice, and hence when to stop.

But however the argument goes, there is surely an obvious, indeed traditional, domain-general candidate for the "success" of a cognitive system: that the beliefs that its operations arrive at should by and large be *true*. It seems not a wildly radical suggestion that truth is cognition's proprietary virtue, *however* it turns out that the architecture of cognition is organized.

I suspect that Cosmides and Tooby would not be impressed with this. For, they might reply, having true beliefs isn't, in and of itself, either necessary or sufficient for fitness. Sometimes false beliefs would serve one better; and, on anybody's story, there are indefinitely many beliefs which, though true, aren't worth having. But if having true beliefs is not, in and of itself, adaptive, then surely there can't be a cognitive mechanism that was selected for the acquisition of true beliefs.

This is a line of argument that Darwinians are fond of. But, in fact, nothing of the sort follows even on their own premises. The point to keep an eye on is this: It is not necessary, in order that evolution select a mechanism, that its proper functioning should be per se "correlated with fitness." All that is required is that fitness is increased *when its function is exercised in interaction with the other properties of the organism.* It's fit *organisms* that get selected, not fit *organs.*

Having hands is, no doubt, a Very Good Thing; but it's hard to imagine that they'd be much use if hands were *all* one had. Well, likewise, it seems perfectly possible that the kind of mental architecture that maximizes behavioral adaptivity is also one that institutes a psychological division of labor: Perhaps a cognitive system that is specialized for the fixation of true beliefs interacts with a conative system that is specialized to figure out how to get what one wants from the world that the beliefs are true of. Presumably, neither of these mechanisms would operate to increase fitness *lacking the operation of the other.* It's generally not much use knowing how the world is unless you are able to act on what you know *(mere knowing* won't even get you tenure; you've got to *publish).* And it's generally not much use knowing how to act on one's belief that the world is so-and-so unless the world *is* so-and-so. That being so, there's no obvious selectional advantage to *either* pure *or* practical reason per se. But put the two together and you have rational actions predicated on true beliefs, which is likely to get you lots of children. (I'm told that's what hunter-gatherers liked. *De gustibus non disputandum est.*)

In short, if acquiring true beliefs isn't adaptive in and of itself (and if Darwinism is assumed for the sake of the argument) then the conclusion we're entitled to is disjunctive: *either* (disjunct 1) evolution didn't select for a mechanism that acquires true beliefs as such, *or* (disjunct 2) if it did, then the adaptivity of this mechanism must have depended on its interactions with others of the creature's faculties; ones that were, by assumption, *not* primarily interested in truth as such. (Which such kinds of interactions would have been adaptive might then have depended on trade-offs that were, for all we know, quite sensitive to specifics of the local ecology; see above.) As far as I can tell, there is nothing obviously wrong with disjunct 2, so it's perfectly coherent, even for a Darwinian, to claim all of the following: that finding out truths is the characteristic virtue of cognition; that possessing this virtue was what the cognitive architecture of our minds was selected for; *and* that for a mind to have our kind of cognitive architecture is adaptive only in case it has a lot of other stuff as well.

I don't mean to go on about this, but it's a widely advertised piece of neo-Darwinist anti-intellectualism (see, e.g., Patricia Churchland 1987) that "looked at from an evolutionary point of view, the principal function of nervous systems is to get the body parts where they should be in order that the organism may survive. . . . Truth, whatever that is, definitely takes the hindmost." The consequence has been a long-standing alliance between Psychological Darwinism and Pragmatism (see, e.g., Dewey 1922), all of which us Enlightenment Rationalists find simply appalling. To repeat: there is nothing in the "evolutionary," or the "biological," or the "scientific" worldview that shows, *or even suggests,* that the proper function of cognition is other than the fixation of true beliefs. This characterization of the (alleged) proper function of cognition is, however, "domain general" on the face of it. So Cosmides and Tooby can't have the premise that "there is no domain-independent criterion of [cognitive] success or failure" for free; they need to argue for it. But they have, as far as I know, no such argument on offer.[13]

Reason 2: "Many relationships necessary to the successful regulation of action cannot be observed by any individual during his or her lifetime. . . . [But domain general architectures] are limited to knowing what can be validly derived by general processes from perceptual information. Domain-specific mechanisms are not limited in this way" (Cosmides and Tooby 1994, p. 92). This sounds like a good old-fashioned poverty of the stimulus argument for innate content; and, of course, I always take those sorts of arguments seriously. On the other hand, here's where some of the distinction mongering earlier in this chapter pays off a bit: poverty of the stimulus arguments militate for *innateness,* not for *modularity.* The domain-specificity and encapsulation of a cognitive mechanism on the one hand, and its innateness on the other, are orthogonal properties. You can thus have perfectly general learning mechanisms that are born knowing a lot, and you can have fully encapsulated mechanisms (e.g., reflexes) that are literally present at birth, but that don't know about anything except what proximal stimulus to respond to and what proximal response to make to it. As far as I know, all the intermediate options are likewise open, at least in principle. The long and short is: you can have a poverty of the stimulus argument for *nativist theories* as opposed to *empiricist theories,* but you can't have a poverty of the stimulus argument for *modular* mechanisms versus mechanisms of *"general learning."*[4] "Poverty of the stimulus" isn't the right *kind* of premise from which to argue that kind of conclusion.

I should add that Reason 2 appears to have a subtext that, however, I don't claim to understand. The idea seems to be that, though the available stimulations may be too impoverished for a general learning mechanism to notice adaptively relevant correlations among them, "natural selection *can [sic]* detect these statistical relationships." This is because "natural selection does not work by inference or simulation. It takes the real problem, runs the experiment, and retains those design features that lead to the best available outcome. . . . [It] 'counts up' the results of alternative designs operating in the real world . . . and weights the statistical distribution of their consequences. . ." (pp. 93–94). As I say, I don't really understand this; but, whatever exactly it means, it sure doesn't sound to me much like Darwin. Suppose, per hypotheses, that the causal consequences of its being the case that *P aren't* such as to affect individual phenotypes in a certain kind of organism. If so, then evolution *can't* sensitize that kind of organism to its being the case that *P*. In particular, it can't select creatures of that kind that believe that *P* in preference to creatures of that kind that don't. After all, selection for *P*-believers requires individuals whose (e.g., behavioral) phenotypes are *different from what they would have been if P hadn't been the case.* But there won't be such individuals unless at least some of the creatures in question can detect ecological differences that, as one says, "carry the information" that *P*.

Perhaps, however, Cosmides and Tooby's point is only that evolution is sometimes able to "see" that the phenotypes of a kind of organism exhibit consequences of the fact that P even if the impact of such consequences on the fitness of any given individual is quite small. That's all right, I suppose, but the situation is symmetric since learning is often sensitive to phenotypic differences that are invisible to adaptation. I, for example, have managed to learn to distinguish between, as it might be, Hegelian Idealists and Kantian Idealists; or between Positivists and Pragmatists; or between Property Dualists and Substance Dualists; and I'll bet my hunter-gather Granny could have learned to do so too if she'd tried. But, as far as I can tell, my sensitivity to these distinctions hasn't affected my fitness (not, anyway, for the better) even one whit; and it is likewise unlikely ever to affect the fitness of any of my progeny. Since, in this sort of case, learning can and does see what selection is blind to, there can't be any *general* argument that selection is sensitive to subtler distinctions than learning, or, of course, vice versa.

Reason 3. "Combinatorial explosion paralyzes any system that is truly domain-general." "A domain-general . . . architecture . . . lacks any content, either in the form of domain-specific knowledge or domain-specific procedures. . . . As a result, a domain-general system must evaluate all alternatives it can define. Permutations being what they are, alternatives increase exponentially as the problem complexity increases" (p. 94). There are, I think, two points to notice about this. The first is that it commits the same confusion between issues about domain specificity and issues about innateness that I remarked on in discussing Reason 2. Pace Cosmides and Tooby, there is no warranted inference from a creature's possessing a domain-neutral cognitive architecture to its lacking an innate cognitive endowment. Arguments that it must have such an innate endowment are therefore neutral as to whether its cognition is modular. Second, Cosmides and Tooby are wrong to suppose that massive modularity is the only alternative to combinatorial explosion. The most they have a right to is that *either* we have the kind of cognitive architecture in which massive modularity avoids an explosion of Classical computation, *or* that (at least some) of our mental processes *aren't* Classical computations. Given the face plausibility that global considerations of simplicity, centrality, internal coherence, and the like are ineliminable constituents of reliable cognition, I think one really should take the second of these possibilities quite seriously.[15]

The moral of these critical reflections is, after all, not very surprising; working out the architecture of cognition is an empirical problem. It's on the face of it not probable that adaptationist considerations will choose among architectures at the level of abstractness where the issue is *modularity or general purpose computation or some of both.* Too many varieties of each kind are imaginable, the character of the (putative) selection pressures is largely unknown; and it's anyhow not likely that these options are exhaustive. The thing to keep in mind is that, as things now stand, nobody knows how to design *any* cognitive architecture that is plausibly what evolution selected when it selected minds like ours. Since there is such a lot that we don't know about how the mind works (I think I may have mentioned that), *it follows* that there's a lot we don't know about how selection pressures determined how the mind works. If they did.

Having said which, I now propose to do a little a prioriizing of my own. Darwinian considerations to one side, I think that, assuming that modular mechanisms are ipso facto domain specific, the idea of a really *massively*—for example, an *entirely*—modular cognitive architecture is pretty close to incoherent. Mechanisms that operate as modules *presuppose* mechanisms that don't. Given our staggering ignorance of how, in principle, the cognitive mind might be organized, this observation doesn't help a lot to narrow the field. But maybe it helps a little.

Stage 3: An A Priori Argument against Massive Modularity: The Input Problem

Here's the form of the worry. Suppose, as usual, that typical cognitive processes effect mappings from mental representations to mental representations. Suppose that a certain mind contains two modular processors: M1 is for thinking about triangles (so it applies to representations of triangles but not to representations of squares) and M2 is a module for thinking about squares (so it applies to representations of squares but not to representations of triangles).[16] And suppose, for simplicity of exposition, that that's all this mind does. RTM and CTM are in force as usual, so we know that M1 and M2 both respond to formal, nonsemantic properties of their input representations. Call these properties P1 and P2 respectively. So then: M1 "turns on" when and only when it encounters a P1 representation, and M2 turns on when and only when it encounters a P2 representation. We therefore infer that P1 and P2 are somehow assigned to representations prior to the activation of M1 and M2. Question: Is *the procedure that effects this assignment itself domain specific?* That is, is there a single mechanism that takes representations at large as its input domain and assigns P1 to some of them and P2 to others? Or are there distinct mechanisms, with distinct input domains, one of which assigns P1 to its inputs and the other of which assigns P2 to its inputs? Here are the two possibilities; which do you prefer (see figure 4.1)? Clearly the first arrangement is ruled out since, if you opt for it, you thereby postulate a mechanism (viz., BOX1) that is at a minimum less modular than either M1 or M2. That would undermine the thesis that the mind is *massively* modular;

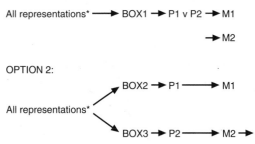

*That is, "all representations" other than those that are outputs of the indicated Modules or Boxes.

Figure 4.1

that is, that it consists of nothing but systems that are, more or less, all equally domain specific.

What about option 2? Prima facie, it courts a regress. In particular, it raises the question of what determines which of the "all representations" are inputs to BOX2 and which of them are inputs to BOX3.[17] Presumably something happens, prior to the activation of BOX2 or BOX3, that serves (formally, syntactically) to distinguish the representations that turn on the one from the representations that turn on the other. (For example, the feature GOTO-BOX2 might get attached to some representations, and the feature GOTO-BOX3 might get attached to the rest.) But now the same architectural question arises anew: Is there one domain-general system that applies to all the representations and attaches one feature to some of them and the other feature to the rest? Or are there two, modular systems, one of which attaches GOTO-BOX2 to some representations, and one of which attaches GOTO-BOX3 to the others? If you choose the former option, you thereby postulate a mechanism less modular than either BOX1 or BOX2. If you choose the latter option, you thereby postulate two mechanisms each of which is selectively sensitive to a restricted input domain; thereby raising the question of how the representations in their domains got assigned the properties to which they are selectively sensitive. And so on. And on.

What we've got so far is, in effect, an argument that each modular computational mechanism presupposes computational mechanisms less modular than itself, so there's a sense in which the idea of a *massively* modular architecture is self-defeating. Just how serious is this? Well, there are ways in which a cognitive scientist could coherently choose to live with it. After all, everybody who is into RTM thinks that there are mental processes that apply *not* to mental representations but directly to impingements from the world. Since, by assumption, these mechanisms don't respond to representations at all, they a fortiori don't respond selectively to a representation depending on whether or not it is P. And since they don't respond selectively to a representation depending on whether or not it is P, their operation doesn't presuppose prior mechanisms some of whose outputs are P-representations and others of whose outputs are not. So there isn't a regress after all.

According to the traditional empiricist picture, in particular, it's the *sensory* mechanisms that block the regress. In effect, your sensorium is assumed to be less modular (less domain specific) than *anything else in your head*. Or, to put it the other way around, the extensions of any categories that processes in your head can distinguish at all must be able to be distinguished in the vocabulary of the output of your sensorium.

(In the case sketched above, the set "all representations" is the output of the sensorium, and, by assumption, it includes some representations that have a property that makes them GOTO-BOX1 and others that have a property that makes them GOTO-BOX2. So, as required, the distinctions that your sensorium makes include [primitively or by construction] *whatever distinctions your mind can make at all*.) That is, in fact, a way to formulate the "Empiricist Principle," of which the more standard formulation is "nothing in the mind that is not first in the senses."

"What," you are perhaps now asking yourself, "has all this got to do with the massive modularity thesis? And why should it matter to anybody whose time is valuable (unlike, it would appear, that of the present author)?" Temper, temper. To be sure, nothing so far should worry a massive modularity theorist *who is prepared also to be an empiricist*; for, though the argument shows that any cognitive architecture must recognize at least one mechanism that isn't modular, that can just be the sensorium; and nobody ever thought *that* was a module. The whole function of an empiricist sensorium is, as just remarked, to be as domain general as all of the rest of the mind put together.

But if you were an empiricist, I expect you would have stopped reading some time back; probably, come to think of it, you wouldn't have started. So let's consider the baleful situation of a massive modularity theorist who is *not* prepared to believe that every cognitive distinction corresponds to a sensory distinction.

Suppose, for example, that such a cognitive scientist is impressed by L. Cosmides and J. Tooby's arguments for an encapsulated, domain-specific Cheater Detection Module (often hereinafter a CDM; see appendix for details). Well, one of the things that's supposed to make the Cheater Detection Module modular is that it normally operates only in situations that are (taken to be) social exchanges. Its operation is thus said to invoke inferential capacities that are not available to the mind when it is thinking about situations that it does not take to be social exchanges. It's claimed, indeed, that you can turn the CDM on and off in an experimental task by manipulating whether the subject does so or doesn't see the situation *as* a social exchange (see Gigerenzer and Hug 1992).

So, then, the CDM computes over mental objects that are marked as social exchange representations; and its function is to sort them into disjoint piles, some of which represent social exchanges in which cheating is going on, and others of which do not.[19] But (following the reasoning previously set forth) this story requires postulating a prior mechanism that responds to situations at large (or, perhaps, to situations represented as involving human activity? or whatever) and maps them onto representations some of which represent the situations as social exchanges and some of which do not. This mechanism is patently less domain specific than the CDM. Query: does it nonetheless still count as a module? And, if it does, what about the mechanism whose outputs turn this social exchange module on? To what domain is it specific?

So far, I've been worrying that regress arguments may show the notion of a really massively modular mind to be incoherent. I'm aware, however, that though there are some cognitive scientists who are fond of such arguments, there are also many cognitive scientists who are not, who find them, indeed, philosophical in an invidious sense of that term. They are, in short, left cold; they are not amused. So I propose to turn to a related worry that is less principled but arguably more pressing.

We've been assuming that there's something in the input to the CDM that turns it on; some property of its input representations to which it is selectively sensitive and that "carries the information" that the current distal array constitutes a social exchange. Question: What feature could this be? How does a module decide whether what it's looking at *is* a social exchange?

Since, Cherished Reader, you are not an empiricist, you presumably do not believe that social exchanges have proprietary sensory telltales.[20] So you presumably do not believe, for example, that the distinction between social exchanges and everything else is somehow implicit in the sensory transducer outputs that they evoke. After all, it's not as though some Lurking Benevolence paints social exchanges a proprietary color. Figuring out whether something is a social exchange and, if it is, whether it's the kind of social exchange in which cheating can be an issue (not all of them are, of course) involves the detection of what behaviorists used to call Very Subtle Clues. Which is to say that nobody has *any idea* what kind of cerebration is required for figuring out which distal stimulations are social exchanges, or what kinds of concepts that kind of cerebration would need to have access to. In particular, why would it be plausible to suppose that a modular, domain-specific, encapsulated computational system *could* detect social exchanges? (How hard it can be to figure out what "the situation" is—what, if anything, the natives are up to—is, indeed, one of the great topics of modern literature. Kafka [passim], Melville [1997], and Martin Amis [1984], to say nothing of Lewis Carroll, all provide examples. Massive modularity theorists might wish to have a browse in this kind of fiction to sensitize their fingertips.)

"Oh, but back when we were hunter-gatherers, Everything Was Much Simpler. Social exchanges were Much Easier To Detect in those days. In fact, almost all of them were orange with gray stripes." Alright if you say so, but I don't see how it helps to make your case. After all, the experiments that are supposed to show that we've inherited a cheater detector module are generally performed on our contemporaries; and what they (are purported to) show is, for example, that performance on the Wason selection task is sensitive to whether the subject takes a social exchange to be at issue. But even if all the social exchanges used to be colored orange, so that Way Back Then the CDM could identify its inputs by their color,[21] it surely can't do so these days. At best, what turns the CDM on these days must be not being orange but rather Subtle Cues to social exchanges. So the massive modularity thesis can't be true unless there is, inter alia, a module that detects the relevant Subtle Cues and infers from them that a social exchange is going on. I repeat the question previously mooted: What is the chance that a *modular* (i.e., encapsulated, i.e., computationally local) information process could draw such inferences reliably?[22]

Here, then, is the long and short: Suppose that Darwinian processes have somehow endowed homo sapiens with an encapsulated CDM that deploys domain-specific inferential procedures (or a domain-specific database, or both) to evaluate what are taken to be social exchanges. Even so, that wouldn't be a reason for thinking that the mind is really *massively* modular, unless you are also prepared to suppose that corresponding encapsulated and domain-specific procedures could evaluate situations at large for whether or not they are social exchanges. But, to repeat, figuring out whether something is a social exchange and, if it is, whether it's the kind of social exchange in which questions of cheating can arise, takes *thinking*. Indeed, as far as anybody knows, it takes the kind of abductive reasoning that, by definition, modules don't do and that (it appears) Classical computations have no way to model.

I should add that, unlike the regress problems I raised a few pages back, this sort of "input analysis" question about *how the mind manages to represent things in ways that determine which modules get excited* is not just "philosophical" but *really real;* it arises in real cognitive science research in ways that baffle real cognitive scientists. I mention just one, well-known example: How does the (putative) language perception module decide whether an input event is in its domain? People used to think (anyhow, to hope) that psychophysics would answer this; there would be some transducer-detected, acoustic feature(s) of inputs to which the sensorium (how that does keep turning up) would respond with a characteristic kind of mental representation; and, ceteris paribus, the language perception module would define its domain by reference to proprietary features of such sensory representations. It's not, to be sure, out of the question that things will still turn out this way. But nobody has found the features so far; and how would this sort of story begin to apply to the perceptual analysis of sign language? Or to reading?

What's especially interesting about this case is that it is *much* more plausible that you don't need to do any complicated thinking to decide that an input belongs to the language domain than that you don't need to do any to detect inputs in the domain of the CDM. That's precisely because language perception is perception, and thus, presumably, is something that happens early in cognitive processing and that is mandatory. Indeed, it's in some part *because* it's plausible that the domains of perceptual modules (like the language processor) can be detected psychophysically that mechanisms of perceptual analysis are prima facie good candidates for modularity. (Just as it's because the domains of putative "cognitive" modules like CDM *can't* be detected psychophysically that they are, prima facie, *not* good candidates for modularity.) And yet it turns out that empirical solutions of the input analysis problem aren't easy to come by *even* in the case of likely candidates like language.

Here's the moral: Really massive modularity is a coherent account of cognitive architecture only if the input problem for each module (the problem of identifying representations in its proprietary domain) can be solved by inferences that aren't abductive (or otherwise holistic); that is, by domain-specific mechanisms. There isn't, however, any reason to think that it can. In particular, the traditional Empiricist treatment—namely, to assume that domains of *all* cognitive processors are distinguishable in the sensorium—is wildly implausible outside perception (and not all that wildly plausible *inside* perception).

So, if it's right that the New Synthesis requires the Classical model of computation, and if it's right that the Classical model of computation works only for local computations, and if it's right that only modularized processing is likely to be local in the relevant respects, then you probably can't save the New Synthesis by assuming that cognitive architecture is massively modular. By all the signs, the cognitive mind is up to its ghostly ears in abduction. And we do not know how abduction works. So we do not know how the cognitive mind works; all we know anything much about is modules.

Chapter 5
Darwin among the Modules

Introduction

Strictly speaking, we could have stopped at the end of chapter 4. I'd promised to discuss the relation between two doctrines, both of which the New Synthesis endorses, which may seem at first blush to be quite independent: that cognitive processes are Classical computations, and that the architecture of cognition is massively modular. The reading I've offered is that Classical computations are intrinsically local and thus badly equipped to account for the abductive aspects of cognition. This won't matter much if cognitive architecture is typically modular, since the more an inferential process is encapsulated, the less it is abductive. But if the massive modularity thesis isn't true, the intrinsic locality of Classical computation is likely to matter quite a lot; it's likely to undermine the claim that the New Synthesis provides a general theory of how the mind works. So it's rational for a cognitive scientist who is committed to mental processes being Classical computations to hope very much that the mind is massively modular.

OK so far. But the New Synthesis is also widely committed to the thesis that "cognitive architecture is an evolutionary adaptation," and you might wonder how this claim fits with the other two. That's what the present chapter is about. My line will be that none of the usual New Synthesis arguments for adaptationism about cognition is remotely convincing. On the other hand, I do think there are reasons why adaptationism should be true of a cognitive architecture *insofar as it is* (massively or otherwise) *modular*. Just as Classical computation needs modularity, modularity needs adaptationism. On my view, the three together constitute a not utterly implausible account of some aspects of cognition. As the reader will no doubt have noticed, it's the part of cognition that *doesn't* work that way that I'm worried about, the indications being that it's quite a big part, and that much of what's special about our kinds of minds lives there.

Here's how we'll proceed. First I offer a disapproving survey of the main standard arguments for adaptationism about cognition. These all turn either on general considerations about the relations between psychological theories and biological theories, or on the central role that Darwinism plays in our understanding of the innate properties of organisms. What they have most interestingly in common is that, if they're any good at all, they are good across the board. That is, they imply adaptationism about cognitive architecture *whether or not* the mind is modular. They also have it in common that they are ubiquitous in the New Synthesis literature. They also have it in common that they aren't any good.

Then I'll tell you why I think there is plausibly an intrinsic connection between modularity and adaptationism after all.

First Bad Argument Why Evolutionary Psychology Is A Priori Inevitable: Consistency

Suppose that adaptationism is true about innate cognitive architecture, whether or not the latter is modular. The effect would be to connect psychological theories about the organization of the mind with biological theories about the evolution of less tendentious organs (the vertebrate eye, the giraffe's neck, and so forth). In contrast, if cognitive architecture *isn't* an adaptation, the right story about its evolution might turn out to be more or less sui generis. It might turn out that good theories about how eyes and necks evolved and good theories about how minds evolved don't speak to one another. In this respect anyhow, biology and cognitive psychology would then be relatively autonomous sciences.

Well, according to much of the New Synthesis literature, that outcome is *intolerable*. It is held to be *methodologically* impermissible. Which does strike me as a little odd. The New Synthesis is, after all, prepared to allow that psychology and botany, for example, actually don't have much to say to one another; let those chips fall where they may. But to suppose that cognitive psychology should not be constrained by the theory of evolution would be "to neglect or even reject the central principle that valid scientific knowledge—whether from the same or different fields—should be mutually consistent. . . . It is this principle that makes different fields relevant to each other, and part of the same larger system of knowledge" (Cosmides and Tooby 1992, p. 22). It is only because "Darwin . . . show[ed] how the mental world . . . arguably owed its complex organization to the same process of natural selection that explained the physical organization of living things . . . [that] . . . in the vast landscape of causation, it is now possible to locate 'Man's place in nature' to use Huxley's famous phrase . . ." (pp. 20–21).

That is all very moving, I guess. But, on second thought, it is both too strong and too weak.

It's too strong because, in fact, quite a lot of what we know about "Man's place in nature" (I assume this means something like "the relation between phenomena that the intentional sciences study and phenomena in the domain of the biological and natural sciences") doesn't actually *seem* to have much to do with evolution after all. Indeed, in principle—so one might have thought—we could know the whole story about how the mind supervenes on the brain, without knowing *anything* about the evolution of either; and that surely would be to know quite a lot about the mind's place in nature. Wouldn't it? So what, exactly, is one claiming, and what exactly is the warrant for claiming it, when one says things like "[Since] humans, like every other natural system, are embedded in the contingencies of a larger principled history . . . explaining any particular fact about them requires the joint analysis of all the principles and contingencies involved. To break this seamless matrix of causation . . . is to embrace and perpetuate and ancient dualism endemic to the Western culture tradition . . ." (p. 21), and so on?

"Golly," one might reasonably say to oneself, "psychology must then be *very* unlike lots of other sciences; because, in lots of other sciences, it's perfectly OK—in fact, it's the usual case—for an explanation that fits a phenomenon into 'the vast landscape of causation' to be largely or solely ahistorical. In the usual case, such ahistorical explanations work by exhibiting the mechanism in virtue of whose operation a phenomenon is *synchronically* caused. Thus, for example, the aerodynamic explanation of how birds fly doesn't, in and of itself, tell you anything at all about how birds *came* to fly. But if it doesn't succeed in fitting bird flight into the causal order, I really can't imagine what would. So, if an entirely ahistoric theory can count as explaining how bird flight belongs to the seamless matrix of causation, why couldn't a likewise ahistoric theory of mind/brain supervenience count as explaining how mentality belongs to the causal order? Exactly what methodological principle do ahistoric psychological explanations violate? And whence, in any case, this sudden onset of methodological a priorism? Are these evolutionary psychologists maybe some kind of Dualists?" So one might reasonably say to oneself.[1]

The argument from consistency is *too weak* because, though it's true—indeed, true a priori—that psychology needs to be consistent with the rest of science, that doesn't buy anything much that's of methodological interest. In particular, consistency is *not* what "makes different fields relevant to each other." To the contrary, mere consistency is cheap; any two theories that are both true ipso facto achieve it. If, for example, you are convinced that your favorite botanical theory and your favorite astrophysical theory are both true, you don't need anything further to justify assuming that they're consistent. Likewise, the laws of quantum mechanics (if true) are ipso facto compatible with the truth that Columbus, Ohio is bigger than Urbana-Champaign. It does *not* follow that quantum mechanics has much to say to demography or vice versa. Likewise, mutatis mutandis, for your favorite theory about how the mind works and your favorite theory about how evolution works.[2]

It isn't, of course, an accident that New Synthesists keep making this curious mistake of supposing that the mere *consistency* of the psychological sciences with biology somehow requires that cognitive architecture should be a Darwinian adaptation.[3] What they really want, of course, is an argument that shows why considerations about human selectional history should matter much in intentional psychological explanation. Accordingly, what they require as the premise of their argument is not that all the sciences have to be mutually *consistent,* but that they all have to be mutually *relevant,* specifically mutually *explanatorily* relevant. That evolutionary theory interestingly constrains cognitive psychology (and, of course, vice versa) would then follow as a special case. The requirement of mutual relevance really does have teeth, and adopting it as a methodological principle would indeed have serious consequences for our view of how the sciences are organized. But, so what? since (to return to the point I made above), it simply isn't true that all the sciences are mutually relevant. Quite the contrary, most sciences are quite strikingly mutually irrelevant, at least as far as anybody knows; as are, for that matter, most contingent truths, scientific or otherwise. It's generally hard work to get theories in different sciences to bear on one another; often, when one succeeds, it's a breakthrough. If, for example, somebody could show how the theory of lunar geography constrains the theory of cellular mitosis, I'm sure he could get it published in *Nature.* But, in all likelihood, there will be no such publication because there is no such constraint, so don't hold your breath. Why should not these banal methodological truisms apply likewise to the relation between theories of evolution and theories of cognition?

It could be true that evolutionary biology importantly constrains cognitive psychology; it may even be *plausible* a posteriori that it does. But the "a posteriori" bit matters a lot. That evolutionary biology importantly constrains cognitive psychology doesn't follow from any such methodological principle as that *all* sciences do (or even ought to) importantly constrain one another. For, at least as far as anybody knows, there is no such methodological principle.[4]

It would be putting it mildly to say that the philosophy of science isn't finished yet. So, perhaps there will eventually prove to be something that's a priori true to say about how scientific theories are required to fit together other than that they'd better be mutually consistent. There could even turn out to be some a priori principle of "unity of science," or of "consilience," from which it follows that biology is relevant to cognitive science in ways that (as far as anybody knows) lunar geography is not relevant to the theory of cell mitosis; philosophy is full of surprises. But, as things now stand, evolutionary psychology can't be called into being by methodological fiat. If there is a case to be made that the architecture of the mind evolved under selection pressure, it's got to be made on empirical grounds. Granny does rather wish that biologists would stop trying to teach the philosophy of science to philosophers of science. She says that she already knows how to suck eggs, thank you.

Second Bad Argument Why Evolutionary Psychology Is A Priori Inevitable: Teleology

It's arguable that functional explanation is essential in the biological sciences and (not coincidentally) in cognitive science too. Indeed, the discovery of facts about functions seem to be among the major achievements in both fields. That the function of the heart is to circulate the blood, that the function of chlorophyll is to effect photosynthesis, and that the function of iconic memory is to hold representations of proximal stimuli until their distal sources can be inferred, are paradigms of successful theories in their respective sciences. It's something like a consensus, in short, that "you just can't do biology without . . . asking what reasons there are for whatever it is you're studying. . . . You have to ask 'why' questions. . . . If [biologists and psychologists] can't assume that there is a good rationale for the features they observe, they can't even begin their analysis" (Dennett 1995, p. 213). The idea, in a nutshell, is that you're not likely to understand how a thing works unless you can figure out what it does; and you can't figure out what it does unless there is something that it does. So: no biology, and no cognitive science, without natural teleology. I don't know whether this is so, but people are forever announcing (in print) that it is, and perhaps there is something to it.

It is, however, the next step in the argument from teleology to evolutionary psychology that I balk at, namely, that the (only?) way to secure the notion of function that biology and cognitive science require is by appealing to Darwin, and specifically, by assuming that the organ whose function one is trying to figure out evolved under selection pressure, and that the function of an organ is whatever it was selected for. (Occasional exaptations to the contrary are supposed to be exceptions of the kind that prove the rule.) "Darwin didn't show us that we don't have to ask ['why questions.'] He showed us how to answer them" (ibid., p. 213). So if you want a theory of cognitive architecture, you need a notion of function; and if you want a notion of function, you have to be an adaptationist about cognition. So the argument goes.

But even if it's assumed, concessively, that you can't do biology/psychology without natural teleology, it is far from evident that the notion of natural teleology that evolutionary theory (allegedly)[5] supplies is the one that teleological explanation in biology and psychology require. The thing to bear in mind here is that any Darwinian notion of function is ipso facto diachronic; it regards an organ's function as intrinsically connected with its selectional *history*. So, if it's true that the function of the heart is now to pump the blood, that's because it was pumping the blood that the heart was selected for way back then. This is, prima facie, an uncomfortable feature of the Darwinian account of teleology, one that makes it hard to believe that it could be the one that biological/psychological explanation requires. Imagine, just as a thought experiment, that Darwin was comprehensively wrong about the origin of species (we all make mistakes). Would it then follow that the function of the heart is not to pump the blood? Indeed, that the heart, like the appendix, has no function, and that neither does anything else in the natural order? If you're inclined to doubt that follows, then the notion of function you have in mind probably isn't diachronic; a fortiori, it probably isn't Darwinian.[6]

Well, but let's suppose, for the sake of the argument, both that you can't do psychology without a notion of function and that the notion of function that you need is, after all, Darwinian. It still doesn't follow that to do psychology you must first unlock all, or even any, of evolutionary history. The reason it doesn't follow is that one can often make a pretty shrewd guess what an organ is for on the basis of entirely synchronic considerations. One might thus guess that hands are for grasping, eyes for seeing, or even that minds are for thinking, without knowing or caring much about their history of selection. Compare Pinker (1997, p. 38): "psychologists have to look outside psychology if they want to explain what the parts of the mind are for." Is this true? Harvey didn't have to look outside physiology to explain what the heart is for. It is, in particular, morally certain that Harvey never read Darwin. Likewise, the phylogeny of bird flight is still a live issue in evolutionary theory. But, I suppose, the first guy to figure out what birds use their wings for lived in a cave. It is (yet another) species of intentional fallacy to argue that if $A=B$, then you can't know about (figure out, have a theory of, explain, make justified claims about . . .) A unless you know about (figure out . . .) B.

Indeed, it seems in point of historical fact that the usual course of inquiry in the teleological sciences is exactly the reverse of what the functionalist argument for Darwinism suggests it ought to have been. What actually happens is that biologists and psychologists are able to work out, from synchronic considerations, a plausible and convincing account of what a system does and how it does it. They then take pretty much for granted the evolutionary hypothesis that the function that they've discovered the system now performs is likely to be the one that it was selected for performing. (I'm open to bona fide examples from the history of biology or psychology where the direction of inference has gone the other way; offhand, I can't think of any.) It is hardly surprising that this is the usual order of discovery, since evidence about the current function of an system is generally far more accessible than evidence about its selectional history. It is, in particular, hard to run experiments on creatures that are extinct.

I conclude this diatribe by remarking, in passing, that non-Darwinian notions of function can easily be imagined. My intuition, for example, is that my heart's function has less to do with its evolutionary origins than with the current truth of such counterfactuals as that if it were to stop pumping my blood, I'd be dead. Maybe it's the case in general that what determines an organ's function is something about which such counterfactuals are true of it.

Third Bad Argument Why an Evolutionary Psychology Is Inevitable: Complexity

"The mind is very clearly very complicated, and Hamlet's sad story to the contrary notwithstanding, having a mind is arguably adaptive (or would have been back when we hunted and gathered). But there is no way except evolutionary selection for Nature to build a complex, adaptive system. Ergo, the mind must have evolved under selection pressure." Books about psychological Darwinism simply can't get from their prefaces to their conclusions without saying this sort of thing; usually more than once; usually, indeed, much more than once. Thus Plotkin (1997): "If behavior is adaptive, then it must be the product of evolution. . . . [N]eo-Darwinian theory [is] the central theorem of all biology, including behavioral biology" (53–54). Likewise Pinker (op. cit.): "Natural selection is the only explanation we have of how complex life can evolve . . . [so] natural selection is indispensable to understanding the human mind" (p. 55). And Cosmides and Tooby (1992): "Selection . . . is the only known account for the natural occurrence of complexly organized functionality in the inherited design of undomesticated organisms" (p. 53). And Dawkins (1996) "whenever in nature there is a sufficiently powerful illusion of good design for some purpose, natural selection is the only known mechanism that can account for it" (p. 202). And so on, *ad inf*; a chap could come down with déjà lu.

For all of which, the complexity of our minds, or of our behavior, is simply irrelevant to the question of whether our cognitive architecture evolved under selection pressure. I do think it's remarkable that nobody seems to have noticed this.

What does matter to the plausibility that a new phenotypic property is an adaptation has nothing to do with its complexity.

What counts is only how much genotypic alteration of the nearest ancestor that lacked the trait would have been required in order to produce descendents that have it. If it would have needed a lot, then it's very likely that the alteration is an adaptation; if not, then not. In the present case, what matters to the plausibility that the architecture of our minds is an adaptation is how much genotypic alteration would have been required for it to evolve from the mind of the nearest ancestral ape whose cognitive architecture was different from ours.

About that, however, nothing is known. (For a speculative but intriguing discussion, see Mithen 1996.) Partly, of course, this is because nothing is known about the cognitive architecture of the ancestral ape. But still more important is this: Since psychological structure (presumably) supervenes on neurological structure, genotypic variation affects the architecture of the mind only via its effect on the organization of the brain. And, since nothing at all is known about *how* the architecture of our cognition supervenes on our brains' structure, it's entirely possible that quite small neurological reorganizations could have effected wild psychological discontinuities between our minds and the ancestral ape's. This really is *entirely* possible; we know nothing about the mind/brain relation with which it's incompatible. In fact, the little we do know points in the other direction: Our brains are, at least by any gross measure, very similar to those of apes; but our minds are, at least by any gross measure, very different. So it looks as though relatively small alterations to the neurology must have produced very large discontinuities ("saltations," as one says) in cognitive capacities in the transition from the ancestral apes to us. If that's right, then there is no reason at all to believe that our cognition was shaped by the gradual action of Darwinian selection on prehuman behavioral phenotypes. In particular, the (presumed) fact that our minds are complex and conducive to fitness is no reason to believe this.

This line of thought strikes me as very much worth keeping in mind when one thinks about the ways in which adaptationism does—or doesn't—constrain psychology. I therefore propose to harp on it a little longer.

In all the paradigm cases of successful evolutionary explanation, it is part of the story that there is a roughly linear relation between alteration of some physiological parameter and the consequent alteration of a creature's fitness. Make the giraffe's neck just a little longer and you correspondingly increase, by just a little, the animal's ability to reach the fruit at the top of the tree; so it's plausible, to that extent, that selection stretched giraffes' necks bit by bit. (So the story is supposed to go. I'm told, however, that giraffes generally don't eat with their necks extended. I do hope that's so.)

I want to stress that the assumption of more or less linear covariance is not dispensable in Darwinist explanations. If changing the physiology makes no change in fitness, evolution has arrived at a (possibly local) maximum and shaping by selection ceases. If changing the physiology a little makes a very large change in fitness, the difference between a selection theory and a saltation theory disappears. (Remember that the standard Darwinist argument for evolutionary gradualism is that large phenotypic changes are likely to be maladaptive, and the larger the change, the greater the likelihood.) To repeat: Darwinism can work only if (only where) there is some organic parameter the small, incremental variation of which produces correspondingly small, incremental variations of fitness. Many of the great successes of Darwinian theory have consisted precisely in showing that there actually is such a parameter in a case where, prima facie, it mightn't seem that there could be one. See, for example, Dawkins's (1996) reply to the traditional objection that random variation couldn't have produced anything as complicated as an eye.

But it is, to repeat, simply and entirely unknown whether the relations between alterations to brain structures and alterations to cognitive structures meet this condition of approximate incremental linearity. This is because, to repeat, nothing at all is known about the laws according to which cognition supervenes on brain structures, or even about which brain structures it is that cognition supervenes on. Make its neck a little longer and a giraffe's fitness is correspondingly increased a little, mutatis mutandis. But make an ancestral ape's brain just a little bigger (or denser, or more folded—or, who knows, grayer) and it's anybody's guess what happens to the creature's cognitive-cum-behavioral repertoire. Maybe the ape turns into us.

Come to think of it, the polemical situation of the psychological Darwinist is even worse than I've made out so far. Nothing we know about how cognitive structure supervenes on neural structure impugns the possibility that quite small variations in the latter may produce very large reorganizations of the former. Well, likewise, nothing we know impugns the possibility that quite small changes in a creature's cognitive *structure* may produce very large reorganizations of its cognitive *capacity*. Turing taught us to take seriously the analogies between minds and computers; and, as we saw in previous chapters, New Synthesis cognitive science has taken Turing's lesson much to heart. So be it. But then it's worth remembering that the relation between a machine's program and its computational capacity is, in general, highly untransparent; very small changes in the one can quite radically affect the other. For a trivial example, it doesn't take much to turn a finite machine into an infinite machine; all you need is one rule that applies to its own output. If you are inclined toward holism about the mind, this consideration should especially interest you. The least it can mean for a system to be holistic is that small changes ramify. If you think that mental processes are global, you can't reasonably assume that local changes will have correspondingly local effects.

Thus far, we've been reviewing some standard arguments that are supposed to show that if you're any sort of a nativist about the cognitive mind, then you ought to be a psychological Darwinist as well. I think these arguments are pretty appalling; that they are so widely influential only shows how politicized questions about human evolution continue to be. Not surprising, perhaps, but none the less lamentable. One does get a little tired of being told by psychological Darwinists that "the biological approach to the mind" or, more irritating still, "the scientific worldview," somehow mandates that their (in fact, quite speculative) phylogenetic theories are true. Maybe Darwinism will turn out to be the right story about the evolution of innate cognitive structure after all; but I doubt that there are any considerations about innateness per

se, or about phylogeny per se, or about cognition per se, that
show a priori that it will. Certainly no one has offered even a
glimmering of such a consideration so far.

On the other hand, I do think that there is an intrinsic connection between adaptationism and the particular kind of cognitive
nativism that New Synthesis psychologists endorse. The rest of
the discussion will be about that.

In the previous chapters, I sketched the following line of reasoning. Start with Turing's idea that cognitive processes are syntactic. There's a plausible inference from that to the conclusion
that cognitive processes are by and large local (e.g., nonabduc-
tive); and there's a plausible inference from that to the massive
modularity thesis. To be sure, none of these inferences is anything like apodictic; they're a matter not of proof but of elective
affinities. Still, I hope I've convinced you that it's no accident that
having once endorsed the language of thought, the New
Synthesis then opted for the modularity of mind.

Likewise, so I claim, there's a plausible line of argument that
leads from massive modularity to psychological Darwinism,
independent of the assumption, previously scouted, that psychological nativists are *ipso facto* committed to psychological
Darwinism. Here's how I think the inference from massive modularity to adaptationism runs:

A module is supposed to be a specialized computational
mechanism, and part of its being specialized consists in an architectural constraint on the information that it has available to
compute with. To a first approximation, each module is supposed to have access to its current input, and to its proprietary
database, and to nothing else. (The architectural "encapsulation"
or "impenetrability" of the module is a name for this restriction.)
I want to emphasize that, qua modularity theory, the kind of
nativism we're imagining thus postulates features of innate cognitive *content* as well as features of innate cognitive architecture.
Each module comes with a database that is, in effect, what it
innately believes about its proprietary computational domains.

Such innate, encapsulated beliefs are supposed to be *substantive* and pretty generally *contingent*. Maybe there's an arithmetic

module, and/or maybe there's a logic module, and maybe what they believe innately is *necessarily* true (i.e., true in every world where 2+2=4; i.e., true in every possible world). But nothing like that could be the general case if the massive modularity thesis is right; if there are to be modules for practically everything cognitive that we do—or, anyhow, for practically everything cognitive that we did back when we hunted and gathered, then a lot of the innate beliefs these modules are committed to must be contingent.[7] And, indeed, this is widely supposed, in one way or another, in practically all New Synthesis nativism. For example, one formulation has it that the success of a creature's modular computations depends on the satisfaction of "natural constraints," or on assumptions of "ecological validity," and that these depend, in turn, on contingent regularities that hold reliably in the creature's environment. Drawing "form from motion" inferences only contributes to a creature's fitness if it so happens that, in the creature's world, points that move together are generally on the same surface. Avoiding visual cliffs only increases fitness in worlds where the appropriate contingent regularities hold between differences of depth and differences of visual texture. And so forth.

A brief aside for philosophers: This is, for better or worse, a glaring respect in which modularity theory is a quite different kind of psychological nativism from what rationalists have traditionally endorsed. Descartes, for example, emphasized a putative connection between the beliefs he supposed to be *innate* and the beliefs he supposed to be *necessary*; it seems, indeed, that he thought that the innateness explains the necessity. Quite generally, the rationalists' favorite candidates for innateness tended to be either logico-mathematical truths or ones that were supposed to be synthetic but *not* contingent (the mind-independence of physical objects, the reliability of induction, and the like). Here "not contingent" means something like "not empirically falsifiable," hence guaranteed ecologically valid in whichever possible world a creature finds itself. Whereas, to repeat, the nativist assumptions that comport with current modular theories of cognitive architecture embrace all sorts of propositions that are contingent by anybody's standards. So a question arises for our kind of rationalists that Descartes didn't have to worry about, namely, what is supposed to account for the ecological validity of such innate beliefs as do *not* express necessary truths? As far as I can see, the answer has to be that they are the products of evolutionary selection.

The internal connection between the massive modularity thesis and psychological Darwinism now becomes apparent. To be sure, as I stressed earlier in the chapter, nonlinearities in the relations between changes in brain structure and changes in cognitive structure, or in the relation between changes in cognitive structure and changes in cognitive capacity, or in both, might quite conceivably lead to massive differences in fitness between the psychologies of even genetically quite closely related creatures. If so, then our minds might have gotten here more or less at a leap even if our brains did not. But what is surely not conceivable is that relatively small, fortuitous changes in brain structure should produce massive increments in a creature's stockpile of true, contingent beliefs. Suppose, as the experimental evidence rather suggests, that humans infants are born believing that unsupported objects generally fall, and that the auditory location of a sound source generally predicts its visual location; and that color discontinuities generally come at the edges of objects; and that objects generally continue to exist even when they are briefly visually occluded; and that the parts of the same object generally move together; and so forth. My point is that having these sorts of contingent beliefs innately increases fitness only because they are contingently true in the world the infant is born into (or, at a minimum, because they are coextensive with such contingent truths in the local ecology). And, barring the rarest of accidents, it's simply not conceivable that a large database of logically independent, contingent beliefs that was formed fortuitously (e.g., in consequence of random alterations of brain structure) could turn out to be generally true. To get the feel of the thing, imagine cutting up the Manhattan telephone directory and then pairing all the numbers with all the names at random. How often do you suppose the number thus assigned to someone would be the number that he actually has?

Only some sort of "instructional" mechanism[8] could conceivably produce large numbers of contingent true beliefs reliably. And, if the beliefs in question are innate, the only instructional mechanism that's on offer as a candidate is natural selection. Nothing known rules it out that the organization of the cognitive mind is a saltation. But if cognitive modules are among the items in the nativist's inventory, then what is supposed to be innate includes quite a lot of independent, domain-specific, contingent, true beliefs; enough true beliefs, in the case of each module, to make its inferences generally sound in the module's proprietary domain. Innate modules thus require a detailed epistemic fit between what's in the mind and what's in the world. Only a correspondingly detailed instruction of the mind by the world could possibly produce that, since we may assume with confidence that the world is prior to the mind.

It is, by the way, an irony of the history of cognitive science that knowledge of natural language, which was the first and is still the perhaps best candidate for being a module,[9] happens to be thoroughly atypical of the usual relation between innate content and natural selection. Like all modules, the language organ is supposed to have a built-in body of contingent, domain-specific information at its disposal; and, as usual, access to beliefs, innate or otherwise, can be supposed to increase fitness reliably only if the beliefs are true. Normally this consideration raises the question that I asked above: how—by what mechanism—does phylogeny bring about the required correspondence between contingent information in the module and contingent facts in the world? How does phylogeny ensure that what the module believes is generally true? I've been suggesting that the answer to this question must invoke some sort of an instructional process (some sort of process in which beliefs are shaped by experience); and, de facto, natural selection is the only candidate if the module is innate.

But now consider the putative language organ, and let's suppose that what it innately believes is expressed by a "General

Linguistic Theory," that is, by a specification of the universal constraints on natural languages (see chapter 1). The general principle applies, of course, that what's innate is worth having only if
it's true. If a human infant happened to inherit a language module that says that negatives are formed by uttering affirmatives
backwards, then (all else equal) the infant's fitness would to that
extent not be enhanced by its genetic endowment. For, as a matter of fact, negatives aren't formed that way in any language that
human beings speak; a fortiori they will not be formed that way
in the language that the infant has to learn. So, in the case of the
language organ as elsewhere, the question arises by what phylogenetic process the module could have acquired the relevant
complement of contingent truths.

However, in the language case, in contrast to the others, the
answer does not need to invoke an instructional mechanism by
whose operation contingent facts about the world can shape the
content of the creature's beliefs. The reason, of course, is that the
facts that make a speaker/hearer's innate beliefs about the universals of language true (or false) *aren't* facts about the world;
they're facts about the minds of the creature's conspecifics.
Roughly speaking, all that's needed to ensure that my innate
beliefs about linguistic structure will allow me to learn the language that you speak is that you and I *are* conspecifics; and
(hence) that you have the same innate beliefs about linguistic
structure that I do, and (hence) that your linguistic behavior is
shaped by the same "innate linguistic theory" as my beliefs
about your beliefs about your linguistic behavior. And, presumably, what guarantees all of these correspondences is that, qua
conspecifics, we have the genotypic determinants of our innate
beliefs in common.[10]

What normally makes one's contingent beliefs reliably true is
that they are formed by processes that are sensitive to the way
the world contingently is. But, in special cases like language,
what makes one's innate, contingent beliefs true is that they are
about the minds of creatures whose innate cognitive capacities
are determined by the same genetic endowment that determines one's own. According to the usual Chomskian story, the

conspecificity of speaker and hearer is what guarantees that what they innately believe about one another's language is true, and hence that their offspring (who are generally also conspecifics) will be able to learn the language that they share. If that is so, then there is no particular need for what the language organ believes to have been shaped by natural selection. That's why Chomsky can (and, if I read him right, in fact does) hold both that human language is innate and modular, and that it is not an adaptation. My guess is that all of these claims are true.

However, if I read him right, Chomsky is also tempted by the massive modularity thesis, that is, by the claim that most or all of our cognitive capacities are mediated by innate modules.[11] Well, if the line of argument I've been developing is right, for Chomsky to espouse massive modularity would not be consistent with his anti-Darwinism. Modules (especially Chomskian modules; see chapter 1) are inter alia innate databases. And—to say it one last time—data isn't useful unless it's true; and only instructive processes can yield true data reliably and on a large scale.

Since innate modules are worth having only if they have access to lots of true beliefs about the contingent structure of their respective domains, and since the world is prior to the mind, there is no way that the required epistemic correspondence between the mind and the world can be achieved unless the world can shape what the mind believes. So there's what seems to me a pretty convincing argument from the claim that some cognitive function is performed by an innate module to the claim that the performance was shaped by a process of natural selection. Accordingly, if the cognitive mind is massively modular— if, that is, the mind is exhaustively a collection of modules—then psychological Darwinism must be pretty generally true of it.

The moral is: If you're inclined not to be an adaptationist about the evolution of cognition, you might do well to endorse the centrality of abduction in belief fixation. To be sure, knowledge of the language of one's conspecifics is an exception to this rule because, in this case, the facts that make one's innate beliefs true aren't, as it were, ontologically prior to the beliefs themselves. Likewise, perhaps, for the innate intentional theory of mind that many of us nativists think people are probably genotypically endowed with. The same endowment that determines my innate theory of how your mind works also determines that your mind works the way that my innate theory of your mind says that it does. And, of course, vice versa. (See, e.g., Leslie 1987.)[12] Similar considerations presumably explain why it's practically invariable in ethology that the most elaborate of a creature's innate behaviors are found to be ones that it directs to others of its own species. But that the inference from modularity to Darwinism doesn't work in these special cases isn't a serious objection to its soundness in the general case. Rather, when you see why the language module and "the theory of mind" module don't have to be adaptations, you see why many other modules almost certainly do.

This isn't, of course, supposed to be an argument that the architecture of the cognitive mind is an adaptation after all. Perish the thought. For, as I expect the reader will have gathered, I think it's plausible, quite aside from the issues about Psychological Darwinism, that the mind isn't massively modular. It appears that much of what the mind does best is "abduction," or "inference to the best explanation," and I take it to be practically a point of definition that just as global processes can't be primarily informationally encapsulated, so likewise they can't depend primarily on deploying information that is contingent and domain specific. Global inferences are supposed to depend on the "shape" of theories, as it were, rather than the details of their content. So the point is not that psychological Darwinism is true; it's rather that, if you doubt that it is, you should likewise doubt that what makes our minds different from the minds of apes is that we have accumulated lots of innate contingent beliefs that they lack. Rather, it's that some radical reorganization of global cognitive structure must have occurred in the process of getting from their minds to ours; and that we thereby acquired our characteristic capacity for abductive inference.[13] There is, as I have frequently remarked along the way, nothing known about the mind, or the brain, or the evolution of cognition, that makes this assumption implausible.

So much for the business of this chapter. I guess I owe you a summary of the main conclusions overall. Here they are:

- A lot of cognitive inferences appear to be abductive. If so, then a lot of cognitive architecture can't be modular. Whereas modules are ipso facto informationally encapsulated, it's true, practically by definition, that abductive inferences are sensitive to global properties of belief systems.

- Because abductive inferences are sensitive to global properties of belief systems, they almost certainly can't be driven just by the syntax of mental representations; not, at least, in the "internal" sense of syntax in which it is constituted by relations between representations and their constituents. For, so construed, the syntactic properties of representations are ipso facto local, and it is a truism that global inferences aren't.

- The internal syntactic properties of representations are ipso facto essential, and hence are not context sensitive. So the more the inferential-cum-causal role of a mental representation is determined by its internal syntax, the less the representation is "transportable" from one belief system to another.

- Even if global mental processes aren't computations, it might still turn out that abductive inferences and the like are exhaustively syntactic. For it might be that they are sensitive not (just) to constituency relations between representations and their parts, but also to syntactically specifiable "external" relations that representations bear to one another. If it's true only in this weaker sense that all cognitive processes are syntactic, then minds—a fortiori, their mechanisms of abductive inference—are still Turing equivalent. But that isn't much of a reason to believe that cognitive architecture is Classical. To the contrary: Classical architectures that seek to exploit external syntactic relations have terrible problems about frames. This is one horn of a dilemma.

• The other horn: The cost of treating abductive inferences in the way Classical architecture treats inferences that depend on logical form—that is, as determined by the *internal* ("local") syntax of mental representations—would be a radical holism about the units over which cognitive processes are defined. Such outbreaks of holism in psychology (as in semantics or epistemology) are invariably indications that something has gone wrong with one's theory. Cognitive science has oscillated between the poles of this dilemma for going on fifty years now, but I suppose that the moral will eventually be conceded; namely, that the Computational Theory is probably true at most of only the mind's modular parts. And that a cognitive science that provides some insight into the part of the mind that isn't modular may well have to be different, root and branch, from the kind of syntactical account that Turing's insights inspired. It is, to return to Chomsky's way of talking, a mystery, not just a problem, how mental processes could be simultaneously feasible *and* abductive *and* mechanical. Indeed, I think that, as things now stand, this and consciousness look to be the ultimate mysteries about the mind.

• Which is, after all, only to say that we're currently lacking some fundamental ideas about cognition, and that we're unlikely to make much progress until somebody has the fundamental ideas that we're lacking. There is nothing in this situation to lament. No doubt somebody will have them sooner or later, and progress will ensue. Till then, I think we're well advised to plug on at the problems about the mind that we do know how to think about. Fortunately, it appears that there are interesting, though peripheral, parts of the mind that are modular, even if there are also more interesting and less peripheral parts of the mind that aren't. And it likewise appears that Turing was right, give or take a bit, about how to think about how the modular parts work. So we've got lots to do that we more or less know how to do. So the massive unemployment of cognitive scientists is likely to be held at bay. Always assuming, of course, that funding can be procured.

If, however, that is indeed the situation to which the first forty or so years of cognitive science have brought us, then noisy celebrations of how fast we've come so far are surely immodest, not to say hubristic. Hubris is in general risky as a policy. It's known to irk the powers that be, and, according to reliable authorities, the powers that be have a very short fuse. Hubris in cognitive science is particularly to be avoided since it is not merely impertinent but also inaccurate. In fact, what our cognitive science has done so far is mostly to some throw light on how much dark there is. So far, what our cognitive science has found out about the mind is mostly that we don't know how it works.

Appendix: Why We Are So Good at Catching Cheaters

There is robust experimental evidence that Ss who are required to check whether P→Q regularly overlook the relevance of ~Qs. So, Ss asked to verify (1), though they routinely want to know what the under-18s are drinking, only rarely remember to ask the non–coke drinkers whether they are under 18 (Wason 1966).

  (1) If someone is under 18 (s)he is drinking coke.

  (2) It's required that if someone is under 18 (s)he drinks coke.[1]

By contrast, Ss who are told that (2) is a regulation and asked to check whether everyone is in compliance reliably remember to ask anyone not drinking coke how old (s)he is. It appears that what sort of drinking is going on is somehow more salient if you're evaluating (2) than if you're evaluating (1). Why on earth is that?

One explanation, recently widely bruited, is that we are innately equipped with special, domain-specific, modular mechanisms for cheater detection, and that these mechanisms are better at their job than the other circuits we use for coping with hypotheticals. (See Cosmides and Tooby [1992] and references therein.) The reason we have this high-performance equipment available, it is further explained, is that it would have been useful for us to have it back when we were heavily into hunting and gathering. (A similar theory would account for our uncanny innate ability to navigate according to the earth's magnetic field—*such* a comfort if you're driving home late from a hunt or a gather—except that we haven't got one.) This putative selectional explanation of the data about cheater detection is among the very small number of flagship results that are supposed to provide experimental support for a neo-Darwinian account of the evolution of cognition. So it's of some polemical significance whether it can be sustained.

In fact, there would seem to be a perfectly plausible, if less imaginative, synchronic explanation of the asymmetry between (1) and (2). The key, I think, is the following intuition, which you are hereby encouraged to share: (1) asserts that there's a conditional relation between P and Q (namely, that Q is true if P is). P is thus one of the relata between which (1) says that this conditional relation obtains, (the other being, of course, Q). By contrast, what (2) prohibits isn't anything conditional at all. Rather, (2) categorically prohibits Q, though, to be sure, it imposes its categorical ban on Q only in case that P. It's thus the whole symbol "$P{\to}Q$" that expresses what is asserted by (1). But it's only the "Q" part that expresses what is prohibited by (2). All P does in (2) is determine *on whom the prohibition falls*. If this intuition about the parsing of (2) is correct, then it's hardly surprising that Ss who fail to see non–coke drinkers as ipso facto prospective falsifiers of (1), are perfectly able to see non–coke drinkers as ipso facto prospective violators of (2). It is, to repeat, precisely non–coke drinking that (2) prohibits.

So the mystery about cheater detecting vanishes if we can make it plausible that, whereas in some sense (1) is about its being the case that if P then Q, (2) is about Q's being mandatory. And it is, in fact, plausible that (1) and (2) differ in just this way. That they do so is built into a difference between the logic of indicative and deontic conditionals; that is, between conditionals that assert truths and those that impose obligations.

Here's a sketch of an argument showing that, whereas it's common ground that "if P then Q" asserts $P{\to}Q$, "it's required that if P then Q" requires Q rather than $P{\to}Q$.[2]

> *i.* Assume, for reductio, that "it's required that if P then Q" is equivalent to *required ($P{\to}Q$).*
> *ii.* Assume *(required $P{\to}Q$) & ~Q*

iii. The inference scheme $((A$ & $(\text{required } A{\rightarrow}B)) \rightarrow (\text{required } B)$ is valid. (If it weren't, *Sam is under 18 & (required (if under 18 → drinks coke))* wouldn't entail *required (Sam drinks coke).*)

iv. Required $(P{\rightarrow}Q) \rightarrow$ required $({\sim}Q{\rightarrow}{\sim}P)$. Contraposition is valid in the scope of "*required.*" ("*Required A*" is closed under *A*'s entailments.)

v. $({\sim}Q$ & $(\text{required } ({\sim}Q{\rightarrow}{\sim}P)) \rightarrow$ required ${\sim}P$ (by *iii* and *iv*, putting *${\sim}Q$* for *A*, and putting *required ${\sim}Q{\rightarrow}{\sim}P$* for *required $A{\rightarrow}B$*). This says that if it's required that $P{\rightarrow}Q$, and it's the case that *${\sim}Q$*, then it's required that *${\sim}P$*.

But (see below) there are counterexamples to (v), so the argument that leads to it must be unsound. And, since the only tendentious premise the argument employs is (i), it follows that we should not read "it's required that if P then Q" as *required $(P{\rightarrow}Q)$*.

Here's a case where (ii)–(iv) are true but (v) is false. Suppose everyone under 18 is obliged to drink coke. Then if Sam is under 18, he is prohibited from drinking whiskey. But *it does not follow* that if Sam is drinking whiskey, he is then obliged to be over 18. In fact, Sam *can't* be obliged to be over 18 because he can't be obliged to do *anything* that he is unable to do. And with Sam, as with the rest of us, there's nothing much that he can do about how old he is (in, alas, either direction). I conclude that Authority cannot mandate the conditional (Sam drinks coke if he is under 18). The only course it can coherently pursue, having taken note of Sam's being under 18, is to mandate categorically that he drink coke.

So, then, we have an argument that, although *it's true that if $P{\rightarrow}Q$* is, as it were, really about $P{\rightarrow}Q$ being true, *it's required that $P{\rightarrow}Q$* isn't really about $P{\rightarrow}Q$ being required. *It's required that $P{\rightarrow}Q$* is about Q being required (in a certain case; viz., in the case that P). Since *S*s know all this, they hear (2) as *mandating coke drinking* (in a certain case, viz., when the drinker is under 18); and since they hear (2) as mandating coke drinking, they see, straight off, that if (2) is being flouted, whiskey drinkers are among the likely suspects.[4] That they do see this straight off should hardly be surprising; if the mandate is "drink only coke," whiskey drinkers are *on the face of it* not in compliance (though, as a lawyer might say, the ones over 18 have secured a variance).[5]

You can assert that $P{\rightarrow}Q$ or you can assert that Q, whichever you prefer. But since you can't *require* that $P{\rightarrow}Q$, you likewise can't *cheat* on $P{\rightarrow}Q$; the best you can do is cheat on Q in case it's the case that P. But that $\sim Q$s may be cheating on Q should, on anybody's story, be more obvious than that $\sim Q$s may contradict $P{\rightarrow}Q$ since, on any reasonable way of counting, $\sim(Q\&\sim Q)$ is more obvious than $((P{\rightarrow}Q)\&\sim Q){\rightarrow}\sim P$. It's plausibly these logical truisms, and not whatever it was that happened to Granny and Gramps on their way to the savannah, that explain why we are so good at detecting cheaters (compared, anyhow, with how bad we are on the standard Wason task).

The received view has it that cheater detection data show that we reason about sentences like (1) and (2) *with different parts of our minds*. The present proposal, not nearly so glamorous, is that we reason about sentences like (1) and (2) *along different inferential routes.* We could hardly do otherwise, considering the structural disanalogies between them that I've just been expounding. In effect, I claim that much, quite possibly all, of the putative experimental evidence for a cheater detection effect on the Wason task conflates the distinction *reasoning with the Law of Contraposition / reasoning with the Law of Contradiction* with the distinction *reasoning about indicative conditionals / reasoning about deontic conditionals;* and is therefore null and void.

Methodological moral: When subjects appear to behave peculiarly in an experimental task, this is not infrequently because they are sensitive to a materials variable that the experimenter has failed to notice.[6]

Notes

Introduction

1. This is not to claim that CTM is any of the truth about *consciousness*, not even when the cognition is conscious. There are diehard fans of CTM who think it is; but I'm not of their ranks.

2. Reprinted in Fodor (1998c).

3. Much of the specifically philosophical discussion of this issue has been about whether minds are "Turing equivalent" (that is: whether there is anything that minds can do that Turing machines can't). By contrast, the question cognitive scientists care most about, and the one that CTM is committed on, is whether the architecture of (human) cognition is interestingly like the architecture of Turing's kind of computer. It will be a preoccupation in what follows that the answer to the second could be "no" or "only in part" whatever the answer to the first turns out to be.

4. Arguably less rather than more, however; getting clear on the nature of the project took considerable time and effort. Particularly striking in retrospect was the widespread failure to distinguish the computational program in psychology from the functionalist program in metaphysics; the latter being, approximately, the idea that mental properties have functional essences. It's only the first with which the present volume is concerned. (For an instance where the two are run together, see Fodor 1968.)

5. Turing's theory was thus a variant of the Representational Theories of Mind that had been familiar for centuries in the British Empiricist tradition and elsewhere. What RTMs have in common is the idea that mind-world relations (or mind-proposition relations if that's your preference) are mediated by mental particulars that exhibit both semantic and causal properties. ("Ideas" in Hume's terminology; "concepts" and "mental representations" in the vocabulary of thoroughly modern cognitive psychologists.) From this point of view, Turing's suggestion that the mental particulars in question are syntactically organized was crucial; it opened the possibility of treating their causal interactions as computational rather than associative. More on that in later chapters.

6. For a lucid introduction to this research program, and to many of the philosophical issues it raises, see Rey (1997).

7. For some of the relations between issues about the productivity, systematicity, and compositionality of thought and the thesis that mental representations

have syntactic structure, see Fodor and Pylyshyn (1988); Fodor and McLaughlin (1998) and Fodor (1998c).

8. One of the unintended, but gratifying, implications of recognizing the compositionality of mental representations is that it places severe constraints on psychological theories of concepts; and among those ruled out are several that might otherwise have seemed tempting. I call that progress. (For discussion, see Fodor 1998b; Fodor and Lepore 1999.)

9. For the largely nonphilosophical purposes of the present volume, I'll be mostly uncommitted as to the "criteria of intentionality" (i.e., as to what it is, exactly, that makes a state intentional). Suffice it that all intentional states have satisfaction conditions of one sort or another, and are thus susceptible of semantic evaluation.

10. It is rather an embarrassment for cognitive science that any intentional mental states are conscious. "Why aren't they all unconscious if so many of them are?" is a question that our cognitive science seems to raise but not to answer. Since, however, I haven't the slightest idea what the right answer is, I propose to ignore it.

11. Mental processes are also classifiable as conscious or unconscious, of course. But I'm assuming that this is derivative; an (un)conscious mental process is just a causal sequence of (un)conscious mental states. (If I'm wrong about that, so be it. Nothing in what follows will depend on it.)

12. There is even a suggestion of a scintilla of some evidence that they may be mediated by distinct, dissociable psychological mechanisms. See Happé 1999.

13. In what follows, I'll often write "The New Synthesis" with caps as a short way of referring to the galaxy of views that computational nativists like Pinker and Plotkin share. By stipulation, the New Synthesis consists of the three doctrines just enumerated in the text together with the claim that the cognitive mind is "massively modular."

Chapter 1

1. This is the nomological sense of "possible." The idea is that, given the laws of human psychology, there are conceptually possible languages that couldn't be the native language of a human speaker/hearer.

2. To be sure, Chomsky's official doctrine is that talk about knowing grammars would be replaced by explicitly neologistic talk about cognizing them in a properly sanitized formulation of his views. This is because he wants, quite properly, to avoid the implication that learning a language is acquiring justified beliefs. (For that matter, he wants to avoid the implication that learning a language is acquiring beliefs at all insofar as the identity of one's beliefs is constituted not just by their content but also by, e.g., their decision-theoretic relations to one's utilities.) But none of this is germane to the point in the text, which is that "cognizing," like believing and knowing, is bona fide intentional. Since cognizing is a propositional attitude, Chomsky's nativism, like Plato's and Descartes's, is a nativism of propositional attitudes. That is what connects Chomsky to rationalist epistemology. (For further discussion along these lines, see Fodor 1983.)

3. I'm assuming, to ease the exposition, that neither P nor Q contains demonstratives or other token reflexive expressions.

4. An argument is "valid" if and only if the truth of its premises would guarantee the truth of its conclusion. Accordingly, it's "formally" valid if and only if it is valid in virtue of the (syntactic) form of the premises and conclusion. If you are a philosopher, this way of putting the idea won't be nearly good enough to make you happy, but it will do for the present expository purposes.

5. Some philosophers apparently think it's an insightful argument against this sort of theory to hoist the eyebrows and say: "You aren't *really* supposing that there are *sentences* in the *head*." "Yes I am," is the equally insightful reply.

6. Note the connection to the idea that psychological laws relate mental states qua states with logical forms. Whatever else it is, causation is presumably the subsumption of particulars by laws. Accordingly, mental causation in virtue of the logical form of propositional attitudes is presumably the subsumption of mental particulars under laws that apply to them because they have the logical forms that they do.

7. By "beliefs, desires, thoughts and the like" I refer (not to abstract entities but) to mental particulars of the sorts that cause behaviors, as when, for example, John's having the thought that it's raining causes John to carry an umbrella. I'm thus following psychological usage, which takes for granted that beliefs and the like have causal powers, rather than philosophical usage, which takes them to be abstract objects (e.g., propositions). This is not to deny that there are such abstract objects, or that they too have logical forms.

8. As with sentences, the constituents of beliefs (/thoughts/propositional attitudes) include the constituents of their constituents.

9. This is a version of the point that Kant and Frege make when they insist on the distinction between association and "judgment."

10. In this respect, connectionism is the degenerate form of empiricism according to which association remains the basic causal relation among mental particulars, but thoughts have *neither* structures nor constituents. For further discussion along this line, see Fodor and Pylyshyn 1988.

11. Descartes thought that the interactions between mental events and bodily events are typically causal, to be sure. But the current question is about the interactions among the mental events themselves (e.g., the kind of causal interactions that presumably occur in reasoning from premises to conclusions).

12. No claims about metaphysical (or even epistemic) priority are implied, though presumably some or other such claims must be true. I wish I knew which.

13. It would be of some metaphysical interest to explain why this supervenience relation holds. The natural suggestion is that tokenings of propositional attitudes just *are* tokenings of mental representations. But, for present purposes, I maintain a meretricious metaphysical neutrality; mere supervenience will do nicely.

14. The idea isn't, of course, that the associative laws are innately *represented*, but just that the mechanisms that constitute a creature's innate cognitive architecture obey them.

15. That typical valid inferences are truth preserving in virtue of their form doesn't, of course, imply that *only* valid inferences are typically truth preserving in virtue of their form. The Turing program in psychology lives in the hope that all sorts of inferences that are heuristically reliable though not valid (and, for that matter, all sorts of tempting but fallacious inferences) can be reconstructed as formal/syntactic relations among mental representations. I think that, by and large, this program hasn't been very successful in practice. The next chapter offers a diagnosis of why it hasn't.

16. To a first approximation, MR is the mental representation "corresponding to" the propositional attitude PA iff (MR is tokened iff PR is tokened).

17. Given the assumption that the representational system that the mind computes in is systematic and productive, CTM is also able to explain why the thoughts that the mind can entertain are systematic and productive too. This is a real advance, not a begging of the question, since it's reasonably clear how the systematicity and productivity of a representational system can arise from specifiable features of its syntax and semantics.

18. To be sure, Turing was greatly indebted for this insight to the "logicist" tradition that preceded him. But since this is not a work of scholarship, I'm not required to mention that.

19. Philosophers will note that whereas "responds to directly" is intentional, "responds to indirectly" is not. This sort of distinction will matter when we get to chapter 4.

Chapter 2

1. This leaves open the quite different question whether the (higher-order) property of having a certain context-dependent property might be essential. Notice that if the property of having a certain context-dependent property is essential, then it will not itself be context dependent. *That* the property of having a certain context-dependent property is essential to *X*s therefore does not entail that there is a context-dependent property that *X*s have essentially.

2. Notice that the principle that the syntax of a representation is among its essential properties, and hence is context independent, transcends disagreements about which expressions in a language are tokens of the same type. Suppose, for some reason, that you would prefer not to recognize that the "John" that appears in "John loves Mary" is the same word as the "John" that appears in "Mary loves John." (Connectionists often do prefer not to recognize this sort of fact. Their not wanting to do so is continuous with their rejection of structured mental representations and hence of the syntactical theory of mental processes.) You might then wish to embrace the view that English contains two different words "John"—as it were, "John-subject-of-a-verb" and "John-object-of-a-verb"—both of which are spelled "John" and both of which mean John. This analysis might reasonably be considered perverse; clearly it flouts plausible intuitions about the individuation of English words. But the present point is that it is entirely compatible with the context independence of syntax. So, for exam-

ple, the (context-independent) expression "John-subject-of-a-verb" that occurs in the sentence "John runs" is the very same (context-independent) expression "John-subject-of-a-verb" that occurs in the sentence "John jumps."

3. From now on, I'll often use "simplicity" tout court as the unmarked term for the simplicity/complexity scale.

4. Lacking explicit notice to the contrary, "plan" and "theory" are just cover terms for any collection of one or more propositions. There's not a thing up my sleeve. For expository convenience, I'll often use "theory" to cover both theories and plans.

5. For this to seem even remotely plausible, one has to suppose that a canonical description of a mental representation specifies, inter alia, the identity of its "lexical inventory." This is because it's plausible that otherwise identical sentences can differ in complexity depending on which words they contain (and likewise, the complexity of otherwise identical thoughts can differ depending on which concepts they contain). I'll take that for granted in what follows.

6. Some generative linguists used to tell this sort of story about how, in the course of first language acquisition, children's minds choose among "observationally equivalent" grammars: The simplest candidate is the one that's shortest when they are all written in canonical notation. But such proposals went out of fashion when "parameter setting" came in.

7. It has, no doubt, occurred to the reader that the alleged context-dependence can be avoided if the simplicity of a belief B is construed as a function that, given a theory a theory T, delivers the simplicity of the theory $T\&B$. That the simplicity of the theories it is added to varies with the values of this function would then be a context-independent property of B (see note 1). Quite so. Still, what determine the effects of adding B to T are not just the properties of B, but also the properties of T. So the contribution of B to the simplicity of $T\&B$ is a function not just of the simplicity of B but also of which T you add it to. This sort of point will presently commence to dominate the text.

8. I'm claiming that this question is left open by the discussion so far, not that it's in fact plausible that simplicity is a syntactic property. (Though I'm officially neutral for present purposes, I'd be surprised if it were.) Suffice it that if global properties of mental representations are determinants of cognition, and if these properties are nevertheless not syntactic, then CTM collapses however you read "syntactic determination."

9. Geographical footnote: Not distinguishing E(CTM) from M(CTM) can be pernicious in other ways too. If E(CTM) is right, then (only) local syntactic properties of an MR determine its causal role. Now, it is independently extremely plausible that only local syntactic properties of an MR can affect its semantics. That's just a way of saying that it's very likely that the semantics of MRs is compositional. So, if E(CTM) is assumed, the natural suggestion is that the syntactic properties of MRs that can affect their causal roles are likewise the syntactic properties of MRs that effect their contents. This is, I think, a root source of the intuition that computational theories of mind comport naturally with conceptual role theories of meaning. (See, e.g., Block 1986.) But whereas it

really *is* plausible that the syntactic determinants of the contents of MRs are all local, such considerations about the globality of cognitive processes as were reviewed in the text suggest that the determinants of their causal roles can't be.

10. That is, some Turing machine can decide whether members of an n-tuple of representations bear that relation to one another.

11. In respect to which, see Fodor and Lepore (1992). The worst-case scenario would perhaps be that the natural units of computation don't match the natural units of confirmation, assertion, semantic evaluation, and the like. If that's so, God only knows how one might even begin to picture the relation between how we think and what we believe.

12. And, if you have the bad luck to be a verificationist, or to be otherwise convinced that semantic properties are epistemically constituted, it then follows that whole theories are the smallest things that meaning, content, and the like are defined for. A verificationist who wants to avoid this madly implausible semantic thesis would thus be well advised to reject the inference from holism about what's relevant to confirmation to holism about *the unit* of confirmation. This point, however, is of merely academic interest, since he'd be still better advised to give up on semantic properties being epistemically constituted.

13. "Everything else equal" means "consistent with coherence, coverage of the data, simplicity and, I suppose, other methodological and empirical constraints that nobody knows how to enumerate."

14. Here and in the next several paragraphs, "theory" really does mean theory, not just arbitrary collection of propositions. Compare note 4.

15. For expository convenience, I've taken my examples of the context-sensitivity of centrality from the history of science. But, of course, cognitive psychology, experimental and anecdotal, is full of them too. Thus, quite a lot of the data that are described in the psychology literature as the effects of a subject's "cognitive strategies" in categorization tasks might just as well be thought of as illustrating the effects of S's changing estimates of which facts about the stimuli so far encountered are central; which properties of a new stimulus become "salient" depends, inter alia, on S's pattern of success and failure in previous trials. "What's salient is context dependent" means to cognitive psychologists pretty much what "centrality is theory dependent" means to philosophers of science.

16. I borrow the term "background" from Searle (1992), who I guess borrowed it from Heidegger (whom I do not, however, propose to read in order to find out). But there's a ponderable difference. As far as I can make out, Searle holds that background effects are a species of intentional causation, and he's right to do so; the background affects the mind only "under a description." But it appears Searle also holds that the background isn't mentally represented. It's RTM in general, not just CTM in particular, that he's down on. This seems to me to make the effects of the background not just mysterious but outright miraculous. Apparently Searle's metaphysics tolerates intentional causation at a distance.

Searle also has a grudge against syntax, which he thinks is somehow not objective. How any relations could be realer than the ones a thing bears to its parts strikes me as hard to understand.

Chapter 3

1. The same view is expressed in *The Modularity of Mind* (Fodor 1983), which, over the years, a number of commentators have paraphrased as saying that "only modular cognition can be studied scientifically." MOM didn't, of course, say that; and neither do I. Quite aside from the difficulty of making clear how studying a thing "scientifically" is supposed to be distinguished from just studying it, how on earth would I know what people cleverer than I am will eventually be able to figure out?

2. Not that I'm exactly sure what a potato future is, or of which potatoes have them. But I don't imagine the details of the examples matter much.

3. Slightly better: It's an instruction that tells the appropriate effector mechanisms to produce the behavior. The reader may begrudge the text its running equivocation between, on the one hand, mental representations that figure (e.g., causally) in mental processes, and, on the other hand, representations of such representations that figure in psychological explanations of such processes. But I would regard such a complaint as churlish.

4. I've generally taken it as definitional throughout the discussion that "computational" means "local/Classical computation." This is just terminology, and it really doesn't matter. We need one sense of "computational process" that's Classical (hence local) by stipulation, and one that isn't; just as we need one sense of "architectural process" that is Classical (hence local) by stipulation and one that isn't. Readers so inclined are invited to subscript as required. I'll from time to time use "computation in Turing's sense" to refer to processes that are ipso facto driven by *local* syntax.

5. The firing probability of a node at a time is also sensitive to the element's "current threshold" (which may or may not itself be viewed as labile). Cf. Hume: some Ideas are "relatively vivid," and hence relatively easy for their associates to activate. For present purposes, we can ignore this, so we will.

6. Or, in "back propagation" versions, of the frequency with which entertaining the Ideas in sequence has led to reinforcement.

7. If it turns out that nodes are neurons, then, of course, parts of neurons will be parts of nodes. But, in that sense of "part of," the parts of a node, and even the fact that a node has parts, are invisible to processes that operate at the level that network models purport to be true of (viz., at the psychological level; viz., at the level at which intentional content is ascribed to mental states; viz., at the level at which nodes get labels). I can't begin to tell you how much chaos the failure to grasp this rudimentary distinction of levels has caused in the connectionist literature.

8. Two expository caveats. First, in some versions of connectionism, it's not the nodes but vectors over them that express the contents of propositional attitudes. This doesn't matter to the present considerations; since vectors are sets of nodes, they inherit the individuation conditions of the nodes themselves. In particular, two networks that differ either in how many nodes they have or in the connectivity of their nodes are ipso facto incapable of ever being in the same vector state.

Second, connectionists sometimes write as though the individuation conditions for nodes don't matter since similarity (rather than identity) is the fundamental semantic relation among representations. But it is never made clear how the required notion of similarity is to be construed; nor will it be. For a brief discussion, see below; for extensive discussion, see Fodor (1998a); Fodor and Lepore (1999) Notice too that the resort to similarity of content resolves the present perplexities about transportability only if similarity of content turns out itself not to be context dependent. But that content similarity isn't but content identity is, strikes me as, to put it mildly, implausible.

9. It is, to be sure, possible to have a Classical architecture that suffers from the same defect; for example, by assuming a semantics according to which the content of a representation depends on its intratheoretic relations as in "inferential role" theories of meaning. It's the main objection to such theories that they abandon in the semantics what the Classical account worked so hard to achieve in the syntax: a type/token relation for mental representations that doesn't depend on context.

10. Good Quinean that I am, I suspect that (outside logic and mathematics) *all* rational estimates of relevance are empirically revisable (rather than stipulative, definitional, or otherwise semantic). I thus set my face against verificationists, operationalists, and creteriologists; and Granny sets her face against them too. You don't, however, have to accept this intransigent view to agree with us that estimates of relevance are *sometimes* empirically revisable, which is all that the point in the text requires.

11. From time to time, connectionists have tried to imagine networks that are able to rewire themselves, hence able to alter their connectivity as well as the strengths of their connections. Given the identity conditions for nodes and networks, this idea is, strictly speaking, senseless. Conceivably, however, a connectionist might model a mind as a succession of networks that somehow replace one another over time. (Likewise, a Classical theorist might conceivably model a mind as a succession of programs that somehow replace one another over time.) God only knows, in either case, what the laws governing such successions would be like. In fact, this is just cognitive-neuro-science-fiction; there aren't any proposals.

12. One might argue that since, in principle, the activation state of every node in a network contributes to determining the activation state of every other node, connectionist architecture is well situated to capture the Quinean principle that any of one's beliefs may be germane to any of the rest. But the idea that relevance can turn up anywhere should be carefully distinguished from the idea that everything one believes simultaneously causally affects everything else. The first claim is what's plausible, but it's only the second that connectionist architecture underwrites. *Anything can* is one thing; *everything does* is quite another.

Chapter 4

1. If memory serves (which, increasingly, it doesn't) some of the taxonomic possibilities discussed in this section were pointed out to me by Professor Elizabeth

Spelke in a conversation we had several years back. If so, grateful acknowledgment is hereby tendered.

2. That is, "without encapsulation or its denial;" viz., theories that take no stand on whether modules are encapsulated.

3. Thus Marr's (1982, p. 325) "principle of modular design," according to which "any large computation should be split up into a collection of small, nearly independent specialized subprocesses" (quoted by Coltheart 1999). See also Tooby and Cosmides (1992), where modules are characterized as "complex structures that are functionally organized for processing information" (p. 33).

4. By contrast, the nativism issue is intimately connected to the kinds of questions about adaptationism with which chapter 5 will be mainly concerned.

5. This means to leave open the possibility that modules *sans phrase* might contain Chomskian modules among their parts. I think it's likely that that is the typical case, as previously remarked.

6. Coltheart (op. cit.) suggests "defining 'module' as 'a cognitive system whose application is domain specific . . . a cognitive system is domain specific if it only responds to stimuli of a particular class" (p. 118). The trouble is that, barring an independently characterized (and motivated) notion of "stimulus class," *every* "cognitive system" is trivially domain specific according to this criterion.

7. I say this is a reasonable guess; but only modulo a really whopping ceteris paribus clause. You can't use MP to assess the validity of an inference until you have are able to *recognize* the form of the inference. And it's perfectly possible that the domain of an argument affects how easy it is to recognize its form. Maybe, for example, it is intrinsically harder to do so in the case of arguments about numbers than in the case of arguments about liquids, or vice versa. Then one might get domain-specific effects on the computational assessment of (i) and (ii), even though they are in fact assessed as instances of the same form of argument.

8. If the distinction between "logical" and "nonlogical" vocabulary is principled, so too is the notion of specifying a kind of inference with "full generality." But, of course, there are indefinitely many ways in which a kind of inference might be specified with *less* than full generality. For example, (iii) might be recast as: "a number is F; if a number is F then that number is G; therefore the number is G." So formulated, it would govern inferences about numbers at large, not just inferences about the number 2.

9. I want to emphasize that this can at best serve only as an informal way to introduce a notion of domain specificity. In particular, it presupposes what we patently haven't got: a prior and motivated way of individuating problem domains. I don't suppose it will surprise the reader much to hear that "domain" and "domain specific" must be defined either together or not at all.

10. It's perhaps tendentious to describe this case as bona fide informational encapsulation. One might prefer to say that a mind that uses (iii) to assess (ii) has really got not encapsulated access to MP but rather free access to a domain-specific version of an instance of MP. But I prefer to think of informational encapsulation as an architectural arrangement that can perhaps be achieved in lots of different ways, of which this kind of domain specificity may, or may not,

be the most important. My reason is that I suspect that encapsulated cognition exhibits much the same virtues and liabilities by whatever means the encapsulation is effected. In any case, it is a question of great interest in which (if either) of these ways encapsulation is actually achieved by cognitive system.

11. Cf. Pylyshyn's notion that architectural arrangements are ipso facto not "cognitively penetrable."

12. This is much the picture proposed in MOM, where I suggested that a number of other interesting properties of cognitive mechanisms often cluster with encapsulation. This too still strikes me as plausible.

13. For discussion of other Darwinist arguments about whether the function of cognition is to find truth, see Fodor (1998c), especially chapter 16.

14. I'm assuming, for purposes of the discussion, that the notion of a general learning mechanism is otherwise intelligible. I can't imagine assuming so for any other purposes; but that, of course, is a different criticism from the ones Cosmides and Tooby offer.

15. Compare Sperber (in Hirschfeld and Gelman 1994, p. 63):

> Fodor [sees] the frame problem as indissolubly linked to the nonmodularity and to the rationality of thought. The frame problem, qua psychological problem, is being overestimated. Two psychological hypotheses allow us to reduce it to something tractable. First, the modularity of thought hypothesis, as pointed out by Tooby and Cosmides . . . considerably reduces the range of data and procedures that may be invoked in any given conceptual task. Second, the hypothesis that cognitive processes tend to maximize relevance . . . radically narrows down the actual search space for any conceptual task.

But only embracing *massive* modularity would eliminate the frame problem, and the cost of that is denying the role of simplicity (and such) in quotidian belief fixation. The moral I draw is thus precisely opposite to the one that Sperber says I do: It *can't* be that the frame problem is indissolubly linked to rationality; rather, what it appears to be indissolubly linked to is the assumption that cognitive processes in general are computations.

As for a theory of relevance, saying that if we had one it would solve the frame problem is as pointless as saying that if we solved the frame problem, that would give us a theory of relevance: Both are true, of course, because "assessing relevance" and "framing" are two terms for the same thing. (Once there was a worm who fell in love with a conspecific. "Marry me," he said "and we can then live happily forever after." "Don't be silly," the conspecific replied, "I'm your other end.") If cognition is to attain true beliefs with any efficiency, it's got to be the case both that what's importantly relevant is generally in the frame, and that what's not importantly relevant generally isn't. Maybe meeting these conditions is tractable within the assumptions of Classical theories, but I don't know of any current proposal for a cognitive architecture, Classical or otherwise, that seems likely to tract it.

16. Read "representation of _____" as extensional for the "_____" position.
17. If all "representations" were to go to *both* BOX2 *and* BOX3, then we're back to option 1; that is, BOX2 and BOX3 would both be less modular than either M1 or M2, contrary to massive modularity.
18. The presumed cheater detection mechanism has for some time been the flagship example of a cognitive module; one that (unlike the visual perception system, or the language-using system, or the system that integrates motor behavior) is specialized for a proprietary kind of *reasoning*. However, it is now pretty clear that as things now stand the experimental results that were offered as evidence that such a system exists are artifacts. See the appendix (also Sperber et al. 1995).

In fact, as Tooby and Cosmides themselves remark (1992, c. pp. 58–59), practically all of the evidence for modular cognition that could reasonably be characterized as not very widely in dispute comes from the study of language and perception. And, even there, the plurality of the cognitive science community that doesn't dispute it is pretty modest. So it's no surprise that most of the arguments about the modularity, or otherwise, of thinking (as opposed to perceiving) tend toward the a priori.

There's really very little relevant data either way.
19. This is all supposed to be de dicto. So a better formulation would be "some of which represent what are taken to be social exchanges *as* social exchanges in which some cheating is going on, and others of which do not represent what are taken to be social exchanges as social exchanges in which some cheating is going on." This way of putting the case is, however, cumbersome even by my lax standards.

Keeping the de res and the de dictos sorted out is often very important when one is discussing propositional attitudes, cognitive mechanisms, and the like; so, at the risk of infuriating the reader, I propose to continue inserting disambiguating footnotes as we go along.
20. That is, that the distinction between social exchanges and everything else is coextensive with some sensory distinction.
21. In fact, assuming this doesn't help. *Being orange* and *being a social situation* are, of course, different properties even if they happened to be locally coextensive Back Then (even if they happen to be coextensive now, for that matter). By hypothesis, what evolved was a cheater detector whose input represents situations as instantiations of *social exchange*, not (just) as instantiations of *orange*. Patently, the story about social situations being orange in the old days doesn't explain how that could have happened.

Sometimes I think evolutionary psychology is all one long intentional fallacy (see note 18, chapter 1).
22. A passage from Sperber (1989) illustrates how easy it is for a massive modularity enthusiast to overlook the difficulties that the problem of input analysis raises. Modules, Sperber says, "process all and only representations where their very own concept occurs. . . . They are otherwise blind to the other conceptual properties of the representation they process. . . . [G]enerally, the presence of

specific concepts in a representation determines what modules will be acti-
vated. . . " (p. 49). However, nothing is said about how quite abstract concepts
("social exchange" and the like) come to be in the module's input representations in the first place; in particular, nothing is said about how they could be reliably detected by inferences none of which is abductive.

Chapter 5

1. It might nonetheless be insisted that merely ahistorical explanations of, for
example, bird flight are ipso facto incomplete. For all I know, this may be true;
indeed, it may be truistic. I can't tell since I have no idea what a complete explanation of bird flight (or of anything else) would be like. Indeed, I'm uncertain
whether there could be such a thing, or, if there could be, what on earth one
might want one for. As far as I know, the literature in which complete explanations are assumed to be what science aims at doesn't ever stop to say.
   For what it's worth, I suspect that explanation is much too pragmatic a notion
to permit the formulation of general conditions for complete ones.
2. Cosmides and Tooby have a footnote that suggests that they are sort of
aware of this. It says that what they really want from the unification of the natural and social sciences is just "the commonsense meaning of mutual consistency and relevance" (op. cit., p. 123). But then they need an argument that the
facts of the natural or biological sciences are, in any intimate way, "relevant" to
intentional psychological explanation. Whether they are is entirely an empirical
issue and can't be established by any general appeal to what the "scientific
method" mandates.
3. For some egregious examples of this fallacy, see E. O. Wilson (1998).
4. Arguably (though by no means obviously) it's a priori that it would be *nice* if
all the sciences importantly constrain one another; so, perhaps that's the outcome that we should hope for, all else equal. But I don't suppose that this buys
anything much even if it's true. Speaking just for myself, I can't remember the
last time things turned out to be as nice as they might have.
5. The caveat is because of the cluster of issues that circle around the notion of
"selection for." Presumably, the required notion of function must distinguish
between necessarily coextensive properties (the function of the heart is to pump
the blood, not to make heart noises, even though it's nomologically necessary
that hearts that do the former also do the latter). The embarrassment is that a
notion of function that is based on the usual account of selection apparently
can't meet this condition. For, in general, if it's necessary that As are Bs, it looks
to be likewise necessary that a process that selects As ipso facto selects Bs.
   This, however, is supposed *not* to be the case, if "selects" is replaced by
"selects for" (see, e.g., Sober 1984). In particular, "selects for" is stipulated to be
opaque to the substitution of nomologically coextensive predicates. So far, so
good. But it is then unclear that a Darwinian theory of adaptation does, or even
can, provide a notion of *selection for* that differs from the standard notion of
selection in this way. (For much discussion, see Fodor 1990, chapter 3.)

It's worth noting that there are perfectly respectable evolutionary theorists who hold that the only thing that's ever selected, for or otherwise, is the overall fitness of whole organisms. Thus the evolutionary geneticist Alan Robertson cautions that to claim that the variation of some or other phenotypic property affects fitness is to presuppose a decision about how phenotypic properties are to be individuated; and that, in the general case, it's quite unclear how to motivate such decisions:

> [W]e analyze the effect of variation in a particular measurement or characteristic with all others held equal. This is a nice trick for the statistician, but rather difficult for the animal itself to perform. When one asks "what other characteristics are we holding equal?" it becomes clear that this is really a completely abiological point of view. . . . [If I'm asked] how do I decide that the . . . observed relationship between a phenotypic measurement and fitness is normalizing in consequences or not? I have to give the simple answer that I do not know how to do it. (Robertson 1968, pp. 13–14)

(I am indebted to Prof. H. Allen Orr for having called my attention to the work of Robertson and the "Edinburgh School.")

6. As far as I can tell, Darwinians hardly ever consider the possibility that the notion of function that biology needs is synchronic and hence not one that adaptationism could, even in principle, reconstruct. They often write, indeed, as though the possibility of some non-Darwinian construal of function had literally never occurred to them. Here, for one example among myriads, is C&T's (1992, pp. 57–58) outraged rebuttal of Lewontin's suggestion that "[h]uman cognition may have developed as the purely epiphenomenal consequence of the major increase in brain size which, in fact, may have been selected for quite other reasons." Is Lewontin, C&T ask rhetorically, unable to "detect in human thought and behavior something more than sheer accident? . . . High degrees of functionality are all very well for eyes, intestines, and immune systems, but what about the constituent structure of human psychological architecture?"

But their passion is not the point unless it's taken for granted that functionality must be construed historically rather than synchronically. The only conclusion to which C&T's argument actually entitles them is that either Lewontin is wrong about the phylogeny of mind or, if he's not, then the function of the mind (assuming it has one) is not determined by its selectional history. What, exactly, is wrong with the second disjunct?

For a recent discussion of some non-Darwinian options, for developing a theory of natural teleology, see Koons (1998).

7. It makes no difference to this point whether the format in which these contingent truths are expressed is supposed to be "declarative" or "procedural." I'll ignore this issue for the purposes at hand.

8. For the distinction between processes that shape the gene pool by "instruction" and ones that do so by selecting among a preexisting menu of options, see Piatelli (1989). It helps to maximize the ambient terminological confusion that

"natural selection" is a mechanism of instructional change according to this way of talking; whereas, preformationist theories count as, in this sense, "selectional." Ah, well.

9. However, there is a new contender for "best example of a module": the apparently domain-specific, encapsulated mechanism that many vertebrates, people included, use to recover from spatial disorientation. For some really rather stunning experimental results, see Cheng and Gallistel (1986); Hermer and Spelke (1996).

10. I'm neutral as to what "performance" mechanisms might exploit this genotypic duality for purposes of language acquisition or language use. A "simulation" style account (see, e.g., Gordon 1986) is one possibility; but there are lots of others.

11. It would seem, however, that I haven't read him right. Chomsky tells me (personal communication) that he is strictly neutral about massive modularity. So the Chomsky of the present text is not to be identified with the homonymous linguist.

12. The idea might be that some explicitly represented principles of intentional psychology are computationally implicated both in the integration of one's own behavior and in predicting how conspecifics will behave. Appropriately psychologized versions of decision theory and of inductive logic would be among the natural candidates. (Thinks: "If I [he] want[s] that P, and I [he] think[s] that $\sim P$ unless Q, then, ceteris paribus, I [he] should [will] try to bring it about that Q.") Only the assertoric force of the thoughts would then distinguish deciding what I should do from predicting what he will do.

Of course, not all of intentional causation could be like this; one doesn't consult an internal representation of one's preferences to decide whether one minds Jones's stepping on one's toe. But maybe this kind of picture would work wherever intentional causation is computational.

13. Shawn Nichols reminds me that, if it's plausible that our minds are vastly more abductive than those of apes, it's likewise plausible that the mind of practically any mammal is vastly more abductive than that of the cleverest machines that we've thus far been able to build. There is, I suppose, no definite place at which such quantitative changes become changes of quality; nor need there be, of course, for clear cases to exist.

Appendix

1. "P" and "Q" correspond, respectively, to "someone is under 18" and "(s)he drinks/is drinking coke." The examples may seem less forced if you add "(rather than whiskey)" as a codicil throughout, and stipulate that "drinks whiskey iff doesn't drink coke" is true of everybody involved.

2. For the record: I think what's in the text is an ok argument and that it does indeed strongly suggest that P doesn't belong to the content of what's required in "it's required that if P then Q." But explaining the cheater detection effect in

the Wason task, which is the main point of the discussion, doesn't actually need this argument to be sound. All it needs is the truth of the conclusion, namely, that Q is what is required by "it's required that if P then Q."

3. That (v) is invalid doesn't, of course, mean that every inference of that form is unsound. Inferences of an invalid form may nonetheless be sound in light of entailments carried by the *non*logical vocabulary. I'm grateful to Alan Leslie for examples like: "if you borrow my trumpet, you should give me some tomatoes," from which it does follow that if you don't give me the tomatoes, you shouldn't borrow my trumpet. I take it, however, that it's the meaning of "borrow," rather than the logic of conditional deontic inferences per se, that supports contraposition in such cases. Compare "if I sell you my trumpet, you should be grateful," from which it doesn't follow that if you're not grateful I ought not sell you my trumpet.

4. The other likely suspects being, of course, drinkers who are under 18. Unsurprisingly, Ss evaluating sentences like (1) in the Wason selection task practically always understand that the P-card is germane. (The P-card is the one that asserts the antecedent of the hypothetical to be verified.) S contemplates modus ponens on "If you're under 18, you're required to drink coke"; so, if you're under 18, S wants to know what you're drinking.

5. I have, however, encountered an evolutionary psychology enthusiast who did find surprising my claim that if Ss construe deontic conditionals in the way I've suggested, then they should see "straight off" that whiskey drinkers are potential violators of "if you're under 18, drink coke." He held, indeed, that if they did so, that would be as much in need of explanation as the original finding that the Wason task is easier in the cheater-detection version. If he was right, then of course my labor's been in vain; I've only explained one mystery by invoking another. But I suspect him of a merely tactical bemusement. Imagine an experiment in which S is told about a party where some are drinking and some are not. S is offered for verification "at this party, they are drinking only coke" and asked whom he'd prefer to interview, the drinkers or the others. Which do you suppose he'll choose?

6. Many thanks to David Rosenthal for helping me to sort out all this stuff. He does Ps and Qs much better than I do.

References

Alexander, R. (1998) "Finding purpose in life." *Science* 281, 14:927.

Amis, M. (1984) *Money*. Penguin Books.

Barkow, J., Cosmides, L., and Tooby, J. (1992) *The Adapted Mind*. Oxford: Oxford University Press.

Block, N. (1986) "Advertisement for a semantics for psychology." In *Midwest Studies in Philosophy*, Vol. 10: *Studies in the Philosophy of Mind*, ed. P. French, T. Uehling, and H. Wettstein. Minneapolis: University of Minnesota Press.

Cheng, K. and Gallistel, R. (1984) "Testing the geometric power of an animal's spatial representation." In *Animal Cognition*, ed. H. Roitblat, T. Bever, and H. Terrace. Mahwah, N.J.: Erlbaum.

Chomsky, N. (1980) *Rules and Representations*. New York: Columbia University Press.

Churchland, Patricia. (1987) "Epistemology in the age of neuroscience." *Journal of Philosophy* 84: 544–555.

Coltheart, M. (1999) "Modularity and cognition." *Cognitive Science* 3: 115–120.

Cosmides, L. and Tooby, J. (1992) *The Adapted Mind*. Oxford: Oxford University Press.

Cosmides, L. and Tooby, J. (1994) "Origins of domain specificity: The evolution of functional organization." In *Mapping the Mind*, ed. L. Hirschfeld and S. Gelman. Cambridge: Cambridge University Press.

Cummins, R. (1983) *The Nature of Psychological Explanation*. Cambridge, Mass.: MIT Press.

Dawkins, R. (1996) *Climbing Mount Improbable*. Oxford: Oxford University Press.

Dewey, J. (1922) *Human Nature and Conduct*. New York: Henry Holt.

Dennett, D. (1995) *Darwin's Dangerous Idea*. New York: Simon and Schuster.

Elman, J., Bates, E., Johnson, M. H., Karmiloff-Smith, A., Parisi, D., and Plunkett, K. (1996). *Rethinking Innateness: Connectionism in a Developmental Framework*. Cambridge, Mass.: MIT Press.

Fodor, J. (1968) "The appeal to tacit knowledge in psychological explanation." *Journal of Philosophy* 65: 627–640.

Fodor, J. (1975) *The Language of Thought*. New York: Crowell.

Fodor, J. (1983) *The Modularity of Mind*. Cambridge, Mass.: Bradford Books, MIT Press.

Fodor, J. (1987) "Frames, Fridgeons, Sleeping Dogs and the Music of the Spheres." In *The Robot's Dilemma: The Frame Problem in Artificial Intelligence*, ed. Z. Pylyshyn. Norwood, N.J.: Ablex.

Fodor, J. (1990) *A Theory of Content*. Cambridge, Mass.: MIT Press.

Fodor, J. (1998a). *Concepts: Where Cognitive Science Went Wrong*. Oxford: Oxford University Press.

Fodor, J. (1998b) Review of S. Pinker's *How the Mind Works* and H. *Plotkin's Evolution in Mind*. In Fodor 1998c, q.v.

Fodor, J. (1998c) *In Critical Condition*. Cambridge, Mass.: MIT Press.

Fodor, J. (1998d) "Connectionism and Systematicity (Continued), Why Smolensky's Solution Still Doesn't Work." In Fodor 1998c, q.v.

Fodor, J. and Lepore, E. (1992) *Holism: A Shopper's Guide*. Cambridge: Blackwell.

Fodor, J. and Lepore, E. (1999) "All at sea in semantic space: Churchland on meaning similarity." *Journal of Philosophy* 96: 381–403.

Fodor, J. and Lepore, E. (forthcoming) "Horwich on compositionality." *Ratio*.

Fodor J., and McLaughlin, B. (1998) "Connectionism and Systematicity: Why Smolensky's Solution Doesn't Work." In Fodor 1998c, q.v.

Fodor, J. and Pylyshyn, Z. (1988) "Connectionism and cognitive architecture: a critical analysis." *Cognition* 28: 3–81.

Gigerenzer, G. and Hug, K. (1992) "Domain specific reasoning: social contracts, cheating, and perspective change." *Cognition* 43: 127–171.

Gordon, R. (1986) "Folk psychology as simulation." *Mind and language* 1: 158–171.

Happé, F. (1999) "Autism: Cognitive deficit or cognitive style?" *Trends in Cognitive Sciences* 3: 216–222.

Hermer, L. and Spelke, E. (1996) "Modularity and development: The case of spatial reorientation." *Cognition* 6: 195–232.

Hirschfeld, L. and Gelman, S. (1994) *Mapping the Mind*. Cambridge: Cambridge University Press.

Karmiloff-Smith, A. (1992) *Beyond Modularity: A Developmental Perspective on Cognitive Science*. Cambridge, Mass.: MIT Press.

Koons, R. (1998) "Teleology as higher order causation: A situation-theoretic account." *Minds and Machines* 8: 559–585.

Leslie, A. (1987) "Pretense and representation: The origins of 'Theory of Mind.'" *Psychological Review* 94: 412–426.

Marr, D. (1982) *Vision*. San Francisco: Freeman.

Melville, H. (1997) "Benito Corino." In *Billy Budd and Other Tales*. New York: New American Library.

Mithen, S. (1996) *The Prehistory of Mind*. London: Thames and Hudson.

Piatelli, M. (1989) "Evolution, selection, and cognition: From 'learning' to parameter setting in biology and the study of language." *Cognition* 31: 1–44. 143.

Pinker, S. (1997) *How the Mind Works*. New York: Norton.

Plotkin, H. (1997) *Evolution in Mind*. London: Alan Lane.

Pylyshyn, Z. (1984) *Computation and Cognition*. Cambridge, Mass.: MIT Press.

Rey, G. (1997) *Contemporary Philosophy of Mind*. London: Blackwell.

Robertson, A. (1968) "The spectrum of genetic variation." In *Population Biology and Evolution*, ed. R. C. Lewontin. Syracuse, N.Y.: Syracuse University Press.

Searle, J. (1992) *The Rediscovery of the Mind*. Cambridge, Mass.: MIT Press.

Sober, E. (1984) *The Nature of Selection*. Cambridge, Mass.: MIT Press.

Sperber, D. (1989) "The modularity of thought and the epidemeology of representations." In *Mapping the Mind*, ed. L. Hirschfeld and S. Gelman (1994), q.v.

Sperber, D., Francesco, C., and Girotto, V. (1995) "Relevance theory explains the selection task." *Cognition* 57: 31–95.

Tooby, J. and Cosmides, L. (1992) "The psychological foundations of culture." In Barkow, Cosmides, and Tooby (1992), q.v.

Wason, P. (1966) "Reasoning." In D. W. Foss, ed., *New Horizons in Psychology*. London: Penguin Books.

Wilson, E. O. (1998) *Consilience: The Unity of Knowledge*. New York: Knopf.

Author Index